"Loiacono invites us on a journey of discovery. On the way, we learn how, where, and why the Interpersonal Psychoanalytic tradition was born and explore its central concepts through the lens of a consummate scholar and exquisitely sensitive clinician. Most importantly, we learn what Interpersonal Psychoanalysis can mean to us. All psychologically minded teachers, students, and practicing clinicians will benefit from seeing the Interpersonal movement through Loiacono's eyes."

Sandra Buechler, Ph.D., *Training Analyst, William Alanson White Institute*

"In this short volume Anna Maria Loiacono describes the origins of interpersonal psychoanalysis in Sullivan's work and its evolution in the contributions of authors who built upon his ideas. The book is valuable because it offers both an account of the development of interpersonal thinking and a vision of the way it is seen and used in a culture very different from the one in which it originated."

Jay Greenberg, Ph.D., *Training and Supervising Analyst, William Alanson White Institute, Former Editor,* The Psychoanalytic Quarterly

"Loiacono's book is an excellent, brief introduction to the interpersonal perspective in psychoanalysis, which has been part of the psychoanalytic world since the 1930s and continues to develop today. This compact overview will be welcomed by senior practitioners, and deserves wide adoption in courses offered by centers of training in psychoanalysis and psychotherapy."

Donnel B. Stern, Ph.D., *William Alanson White Institute, New York*

Interpersonal Psychoanalysis

In this book, Anna Maria Loiacono introduces the reader to the origins of Interpersonal Psychoanalysis, its most important concepts, and their clinical value.

Throughout the chapters, Loiacono navigates historically through the principles of Harry Stack Sullivan, clearly and succinctly outlining the ideas of those thinkers who followed, to the latest reflections of Contemporary Interpersonal Psychoanalysis. Illustrated with case vignettes, this book addresses concepts such as dissociation, differences between splitting and dissociation, countertransference, enactments, field theory, hermeneutics, the unconscious, the unformulated experience, self-disclosure, relational and interpersonal psychoanalysis, change and the use of the therapist's subjectivity, as they are currently considered in the interpersonal approach, seen from the perspective of Loiacono's personal point of view and professional experience.

Part of the *Routledge Introductions to Contemporary Psychoanalysis* series, this book is a vital read for all analysts in practice and training, as well as psychologists and psychiatrists.

Anna Maria Loiacono is a Relational and Interpersonal Psychoanalyst who lives and works in Florence, Italy. She is a Training and Supervising Analyst at the Institute of Analytic Psychotherapy of Florence and teaches in Italian and foreign Schools of Psychotherapy. She is the Secretary General of the International Federation of Psychoanalytic Societies (IFPS).

Routledge Introductions to Contemporary Psychoanalysis

Series Editor: Aner Govrin
Executive Editor: Yael Peri Herzovich

This comprehensive series illuminates the intricate landscape of psychoanalytic theory and practice. In this collection of concise yet illuminating volumes, we delve into the influential figures, groundbreaking concepts, and transformative theories that shape the contemporary psychoanalytic landscape. At the heart of each volume lies a commitment to clarity, accessibility, and depth. Our expert authors, renowned scholars and practitioners in their respective fields, guide readers through the complexities of psychoanalytic thought with precision and enthusiasm. Whether you are a seasoned psychoanalyst, a student eager to explore the field, or a curious reader seeking insight into the human psyche, our series offers a wealth of knowledge and insight.

Antonino Ferro: A Contemporary Introduction
Robert Snell

Transgenerational Trauma: A Contemporary Introduction
Jill Salberg and Sue Grand

Schizophrenia: A Contemporary Introduction
Gillian Steggles

Erotic Transferences: A Contemporary Introduction
Andrea Celenza

Otto Kernberg: A Contemporary Introduction
Frank Yeomans, Diana Diamond and Eve Caligor

For more information about this series, please visit: www.routledge.com/Routledge-Introductions-to-Contemporary-Psychoanalysis/book-series/ICP

Interpersonal Psychoanalysis

A Contemporary Introduction

Anna Maria Loiacono

Routledge
Taylor & Francis Group

LONDON AND NEW YORK

Designed cover image: Designed cover image: © Michal Heiman, Asylum 1855–2020, The Sleeper (video, psychoanalytic sofa and Plate 34), exhibition view, Herzliya Museum of Contemporary Art, 2017

First published 2026
by Routledge
4 Park Square, Milton Park, Abingdon, Oxon OX14 4RN

and by Routledge
605 Third Avenue, New York, NY 10158

Routledge is an imprint of the Taylor & Francis Group, an informa business

British Library Cataloguing-in-Publication Data
A catalogue record for this book is available from the British Library

ISBN: 978-1-032-84475-6 (hbk)
ISBN: 978-1-032-79716-8 (pbk)
ISBN: 978-1-003-51284-4 (ebk)

DOI: 10.4324/9781003512844

Typeset in Times New Roman
by Taylor & Francis Books

I dedicate this work to Giuseppe, Francesca and Giulia, their parents and grandparents, and my beloved husband, Alessandro.

Contents

Acknowledgments

I'm deeply grateful to Sandra Buechler, who encouraged me to embrace this project, and Donnel Stern, for his support and his suggestions. I want to also thank all the colleagues I met at the William Alanson White Institute, for helping me in the ever-deepening discovery of what Interpersonal Psychoanalysis means for me.

I'm pleased to acknowledge Aner Govrin, Yael Peri and Itamar Ezer, editors of this book, for their hard work in its publishing, and all the Routledge staff too, who contributed greatly. I thank also my analysts, and my supervisor and mentor Pier Francesco Galli, who passed away a few months ago; he believed in me and pushed me to study more and more and to write down my ideas.

A special thanks to Arne Døske, Jan Johansson, Sharon Kaufman, Darius Leskauskas, Ian Miller, Michal Pantzer and Robert Prince, "the Dubliners", with whom I share intimacy and passion for psychoanalysis. Thanks also to my peer group, Stefano Fissi, Daniela Giommi, Lilia Gagnarli, Elena Guidi and Michal Pantzer, for the clinical work we have been doing for years.

I would like to express my gratitude also to all the colleagues and friends, and the students too, of my Institute, the Istituto di Psicoterapia Analitica di Firenze – people with whom I have shared the last 45 years; it's been an incredible and exciting journey. A special thanks to Mabel Gotti, who is always close and helpful. I'm grateful also to my translator Joyce Myerson, who helps me greatly.

And finally, many thanks to my beloved husband, who puts up with and supports me in my work, and to my family, for the joy they always give me.

And, last but not least, to my patients, from whom I never stop learning.

Series Editor's Preface

Aner Govrin

Routledge Introductions to Contemporary Psychoanalysis is one of the most prominent psychoanalytic publishing ventures of our day. The series' aim is to become an encyclopedia of psychoanalysis, with each entry given its own book.

Each volume serves as a gateway into a specific aspect of psychoanalytic theory and practice. From the pioneering works of Sigmund Freud to the innovative contributions of modern theorists such as Antonino Ferro and Michal Eigen, our series covers a diverse range of topics, including seminal figures, key concepts, and emerging trends. Whether you are interested in classical psychoanalysis, object relations theory, or the intersection of neuroscience and psychoanalysis, you will find a wealth of resources within our collection.

One of the hallmarks of our series is its interdisciplinary approach. While rooted in psychoanalytic theory, our volumes draw upon insights from psychology, philosophy, sociology, and other disciplines to offer a holistic understanding of the human mind and its complexities.

Each volume in the series is crafted with the reader in mind, balancing scholarly rigor with engaging prose. Whether you are embarking on your journey into psychoanalysis or seeking to deepen your understanding of specific topics, our series provides a clear and comprehensive roadmap.

Moreover, our series is committed to fostering dialogue and debate within the psychoanalytic community. Each volume invites readers to critically engage with the material, encouraging reflection, discussion, and further exploration.

We invite you to join us on this journey of discovery as we explore the ever-evolving landscape of psychoanalysis.

Aner Govrin

Introduction
What Distinguishes Interpersonal Psychoanalysis Today?

In her famous novel, *Memoirs of Hadrian*, Marguerite Yourcenar (1951) attested that one's true birthplace is the one in which a person senses him/herself for the first time. For me, that place – of the mind, naturally – is represented by interpersonal psychoanalysis, in which both my individuality and my professional life have found solid support for navigating life and honoring my fundamental mission.

I am therefore happy to have this opportunity to speak about interpersonal thought, and I hope that whatever the motivation readers may have for wishing to consult these pages, they will be able to find in them a valid reference point in their search for understanding and helping human suffering and the malaise of contemporary society, as was the case for me.

Dissociation, enactment, avoidance, a sense of loneliness, integration – these are the major themes which interpersonal psychoanalysis has examined in order to always better understand human suffering, offering its own way of envisioning the analyst/patient relationship and the clinical process in general.

Firstly, let us explore together how interpersonal psychoanalysis came to be.

As it has been well described by Edith Kurzweil (1989), a large number of European psychoanalysts in around 1930 moved to America, thus escaping to the diaspora. Many of them quickly adhered to the hegemonic psychoanalytical culture of the moment – Ego psychology, thus aligning themselves with the psychoanalytical mainstream then in vogue. Other young analysts and

DOI: 10.4324/9781003512844-1

analytical candidates were instead attracted to interpersonal thought specifically because of its rejection of the rigid interpretations of human life of which the mainstream was standard-bearer (Hirsch, 2015; Stern and Hirsch, 2017).

These psychoanalysts agreed to brandish these concepts:

> ... the inevitable centrality of the Oedipus conflict; the inevitability of the transference neurosis; the insistence on defining psychoanalysis as the application of a single, standard technique in which the analyst as a particular individual should make no difference, resulting in rigid conceptions of psychoanalytic neutrality and anonymity, and a definition of psychoanalysis that depended on concrete matters such as frequency (four times a week or more) and the use of the couch; the belief that experience unfolds more or less exclusively from the intrapsychic world; the death instinct; penis envy; drive theory in general, with its internal, biological emphasis, and its de-emphasis on the 'real' experience with 'real' people that interpersonalists stressed; and the resulting biologized understanding of psychological development, with its theories of libido and inevitable, rigidly unfolding psychosexual stages.

Today most of these positions are more or less discredited, even in the psychoanalytic mainstream. The Oedipus conflict is still acknowledged, of course, but it is no longer understood as the be-all and end-all that it was fifty years ago; the concepts of transference neurosis and standard psychoanalytic technique, including rigid definitions of analytic neutrality and anonymity, seem quaint; the matter of frequency and the use of the couch have been discredited as litmus tests; the theory of psychosexual stages and the resulting theories of psychopathology (outmoded accounts of obsessive-compulsive neurosis, hysteria, and narcissism) are just plain dead; and drive theory, penis envy, and the death instinct, while they continue to be addressed in the mainstream literature, are discussed in a way that is so much less concrete and foundational, and so much more sophisticated and integrated with subtler understandings of their place in clinical relatedness, that interpersonalists, even if we cannot comfortably embrace them, can often live with them. In the meantime, while ceasing to use many of the ideas with which the early interpersonalists most strongly disagreed, mainstream American, Freudian analysts have also leavened their use of intrapsychically-oriented ideas with a much greater acceptance of the significance of the contemporary psychoanalytic interaction and the personal participation of the analyst, particularly her unconscious personal participation.

(Stern, in Stern and Hirsch, 2017)

In short, the spirit which gave birth to interpersonalism, which continues to permeate it, is a libertarian and anti-dogmatic spirit, one that is open to dialogue and willing to question its own knowledge in the light of new scientific discoveries and new sciences in the service of humanity and in the study of the nature of mental suffering. On this basis, the humanistic/existential values typical of this approach (Buechler, 2004), like courage, integrity, hope, honesty and authenticity acquire a certain prominence.

As we will eventually see more fully (chapters 1–2, 3–4), interpersonal psychoanalysis was born out of the encounter between Harry Stack Sullivan's interpersonal theory of psychiatry, which became interpersonal psychoanalysis through Clara M. Thompson (chapter 4), and Erich Fromm's dream theory. In this book, we will only make reference to Sullivan's thought, for his originality in constructing an absolutely unique coherent and structured frame (Fiscalini, 1994). In fact, I have concentrated above all on the typically interpersonal concept of dissociation and on its subsequent implications, which define a specific philosophy of the clinical process (Hirsch, 1990, 1995, 1996, 1998, 2008, 2015; Stern, 2007, 2010, 2015, 2019; Levenson, 1972, 1983, 2018).

The aim of this book is in fact one of attempting to awaken the reader's interest and curiosity, thus inspiring them to further delve into those subjects which have only been touched upon. I have given priority to the ideas of certain writers over others not in order of importance, obviously, but more because these authors, which I have chosen, embody to a greater extent the conceptual thread that I wished to follow, namely the clinic of dissociation, the importance of countertransference, the unconscious and the interpersonal field, the clinical process, and change.

The first part will deal with the conceptual roots of interpersonalism, namely the scientific and cultural context within which it took shape (chapter 1); a brief overview of Sullivan's life will follow and how events influenced the formation of his ideas (chapter 2). In chapter 3, I will delve into the fundamental concepts that underpin Sullivan's thinking, to demonstrate the specifics of his approach in the use of these concepts and in how they are clinically articulated. In chapter 4, we will learn how Sullivan's interpersonal theory of psychiatry becomes Interpersonal Psychoanalysis, especially through the works of Clara Mabel Thompson.

In the second part I will mostly concentrate on the concept of dissociation (chapter 5) and establish the analogies and differences with the concept of splitting and the use of this concept in other orientations, to finally arrive at the concept of the interpersonal field (chapter 6), with some notes on the differences between the interpersonal field and the intersubjective one. In chapter 7, we will dig more deeply into the concept of countertransference and its use for the purposes of treatment, in line with the ideas of Irwin Hirsch (1990, 1995, 1996, 2008).

The third and final part is centered around clinical theory in contemporary interpersonal psychoanalysis; chapter 8 deals with trauma, enactment, self-revelation, self-disclosure and disclosure in the analytical process, continuing with some observations on angst as a "feeling of presence", as a type of feeling that accompanies the processes of integration, and finishing with the use of the analyst's subjectivity. Some clinical vignettes will embellish these concepts in order to be better understood in many of their ramifications. In chapter 9, I will showcase the radical theory of the unconscious proposed by Donnel B. Stern, through his idea of the unformulated experience. In chapter 10, we will learn of Edgar Levenson's theories, with his penetrating observations on psychoanalytic praxis and on change.

In chapter 11, I will touch on many other authoritative contemporary voices representing this orientation, such as Jay Greenberg, Sandra Buechler, Jack Drescher, Mark Blechner and others, who have contributed, and continue to do so, to the development of interpersonal psychoanalysis in an authoritative and impassionate way.

Last, but not least, in chapter 12, I will speak about my own personal way of living interpersonalism in my profession and present specific vignettes drawn from my clinical practice.

Section 1

Chapter 1

The Roots of Interpersonal Thought

The key elements of the development of Sullivan's ideas are based on the psychoanalysis of Freud, from whom he derived his way of perceiving mental illness; on the new orientation of American psychiatry promoted by Adolf Meyer (1866–1950), from whom he inherited the concept that mental illness is a way of responding and reacting to life – a system of behavior; and on W. A. White (1870–1937), with whom Sullivan collaborated in St. Elizabeths Hospital in Washington DC in 1921–22, and in whose company his passion to always pursue what occurs within the patient's soul was nurtured. In addition to these influences, we also discern the pragmatism of William James, the social psychology of G. H. Mead and the ideas of C. Cooley.

The American Psychiatric and Psychoanalytic Context in the Early Twentieth Century

Early twentieth-century American psychotherapy comprised three basic trends: hypnosis, suggestion and re-education.

These three currents of thought were all operating in New England, in the so-called Boston School: Adolf Meyer held his psychiatric lectures at the Worcester Insane Asylum (where Freud had held his five 1909 conferences in Worcester, Massachusetts); William James (theoretician of functionalism or radical empiricism) brought his students here and stayed to discuss psychiatry and the scientific method with Meyer; James Putnam (1846–1918), on the other hand, was Harvard's first professor of neurology and had stimulated James in the drafting of his Principles of Psychology.

DOI: 10.4324/9781003512844-3

The 1909 conferences in America had gone very well, and Freud and Jung had developed important relationships with the psychologists of the new continent, especially with the great elderly gentleman of Harvard (as Ferenczi called him), James Putnam, who invited Freud and Jung to his cabin in the Adirondacks, which reminded Freud of the Austrian countryside.

James, Meyer and Putnam played a fundamental role in the development of American psychotherapy and in the reception of psychoanalytical concepts, as well as in Sullivan's intellectual formation.

Adolf Meyer (1866–1950) was born in Switzerland and had studied neurology with Auguste Forel at the University of Zurich. He had also worked briefly with Charcot in Paris, before emigrating to the USA in 1892 (the year Sullivan was born).

In a few years he became famous as the person who was occupied with all the details cited by patients, for which he attempted to use both the Kraepelinian classification system as well as the ideas of Freud. However, he never practiced psychoanalysis, and over time he steadily distanced himself from it (we are reminded of the events with Clara Thompson at the Phipps Clinic, chapter 4).

He was president of the American Psychiatric Association and was one of the most influential figures in psychiatry in the first half of the twentieth century, an advocate, along with White and Putnam, of what would then be defined as the "New Psychiatry".

One of his core ideas was that mental illnesses were more a product of dysfunctional personalities rather than pathologies of the brain. In addition, he believed that each and everyone's social and biological factors over the course of their life must be more widely considered in the diagnosis and treatment of patients.

Last, but not least, he was one of the first to maintain the value of occupational therapy, claiming that there was an important connection between a person's activity and their mental health. In fact, he coined the term "ergasiology", from the Greek word "to work" and "to do", as another way to classify psychobiology.

He was a convinced empiricist and always maintained the necessity of a scientific approach to the understanding of mental illnesses. Patients would be understood in terms of the "psychobiological" situation of their life. In other words, he saw psychic malaise as a type of biopsychosocial reaction rather than a merely biological entity.

In conclusion, most of the founders of the New York Psychoanalytic Society (the same one from which in 1940 Thompson, Horney, Fromm, Fromm-Reichmann, etc. departed) had worked with and/or under him.

William Alanson White (1870–1937) was born in Brooklyn and studied at Cornell University (where Meyer would become a professor from 1904 to 1909) from 1885 to 1889, graduating in medicine in 1891. From 1903 onwards, he was the superintendent at St. Elizabeths Hospital, which was a state psychiatric hospital, with headquarters in Washington D.C. He spent the rest of his career there. He was president of the American Psychopathological Society, the American Psychiatric Association, and the American Psychoanalytic Society.

During his superintendence at St. Elizabeths, which served federal and military workers and the residents of the District of Columbia, he brought about numerous reforms. Soon the hospital was transformed from a warehouse occupied by insane people into a place where treatment was provided through psychotherapy as well. He ended the use of containment straitjackets and opened a beauty salon for female in-patients.

Sullivan collaborated with White in 1921–22, at St. Elizabeths Hospital in Washington D.C. (see Perry, 1982, chapter 22) for the significance of this encounter). Not only was an in-depth and comprehensive study of each individual patient fundamental to them both, and therefore they promoted the transition from an asylum-type psychiatry to a clinical psychiatry, but also crucial was their commitment to mental health and the professionalization of psychiatry, an exigency that was deeply felt in America at the beginning of the twentieth century. It didn't seem that there could have been a better tool of psychoanalysis to advance this transition, which was something that Freud himself corroborated on his 1909 visit (Kurzweil, 1989).

These are the socio-historical coordinates about which Russell Jacoby spoke in his famous book, *The Repression of Psychoanalysis* (1983).

The Conceptual Roots of Interpersonalism

The sociocultural thread that crosses Sullivan's entire opus originates in the thinking of Charles H. Cooley (1864–1929), who worked at the University of Michigan, and, perhaps more directly, from George H. Mead (1863–1931) of the University of Chicago. Mead emphasized the role of language as a predominant factor in human development. Cooley instead highlighted the malleable nature of humans, which for him could not be reduced to a mere medical-type explanation. Both, however, stressed the importance of the "other" in the formation of personality. In other words, everyone grows and is structured on the basis of how the other relates to us.

This conception is rooted in the ideas of the social philosopher and economist Adam Smith (1723–1790) and the British Empiricist School.

Mead had also coined the term "selective attention" (Rychlak, 1973), taken up again in the Sullivanian "selective inattention". Mead's point of view concerning "selective attention" was also shared by William James, the father of pragmatism, the American philosophy springing directly out of English empiricism.

In addition, it is interesting to note the operational derivation of Sullivan's ideas on *participant observation* (see chapter 7), via the work of Robert E. Park, empiricist of the Chicago School, specifically focused on the research of the empirical laws of human behavior. This influence on Sullivan was so important as to make him select a subtitle for his *Psychiatry* journal: "Journal for the Operational Statement of Interpersonal Relations".

The operational method consisted of defining a theoretical construct as scientific only when it had been substantiated by empirical measures, which involved the use of dependent and independent variables in the research.

Park's predecessor had been William Isaac Thomas (1863–1947), who was head of the Chicago School until 1918 and who had been extremely preoccupied with the condition of immigrants in America, so much so that he had been arrested and forced to resign. In his text, *The Child in America* (1928), Thomas coined his definition of "situation", also called the Thomas Theorem: "If men define situations as real, they are real in their consequences" (Thomas and Thomas, 1928, p. 572).

Thomas' statement has been considered one of the most important "laws" of social science: the social situation would thus be the result of a gradual process through which the subjects involved in an interaction "construct" their own understanding of the interaction itself and its context.

Sullivan also cites the work of A. Korzybski (1921, 1924) and that of Thomas Verner Moore (1899–1924), psychiatrist, educator and Carthusian monk (under the name Don Pablo Maria), who was the first to use the term "parataxis" in his work: "The Parataxes: A Study and Analysis of Certain Borderline Mental States" (1921), referring however only to some very serious states, as Sullivan himself reminds us in his writings on schizophrenia.

Symbolic Interactionism

Symbolic interactionism represents the dominant theoretical approach in the studies of the Chicago School and of George Herbert Mead. His reflections constitute a starting point for the development of social psychology and a progression in the development of the pragmatist theory of William James.

The accent was placed upon the creation of meaning in life and in human actions, highlighting the pluralistic nature of society, the cultural and social relativism of the ethical and social norms and rules and the view of the self as socially structured. Symbolic interactionism is mainly concerned with social interaction occurring in the daily life of people.

Besides the pragmatism of William James and Charles Sanders Peirce, interactionist thought was profoundly influenced by the philosophers Max Weber, Edmund Husserl and Alfred Schütz, and in the linguistic context by the works of Ferdinand de Saussure, Ernst Cassirer, and Ludwig Wittgenstein.

Mead maintained that the interactions between individuals and groups of individuals were not born out of a series of responses to stimuli (a behavioral perspective) but from the interpretations of symbolic meanings attributed to the stimuli themselves. For Mead, the individual lives and operates in a social world. We can understand the way in which individuals act only if we consider their behavior within the social group to which they belong, since the subject's actions transcend the borders of the individual and involve the other members of the group as well.

Symbolic interactionism had its most productive and fertile moment from the thirties to the sixties in the twentieth century.

Among the chief exponents of interactionism, we have Erving Goffman, who applied a dramaturgical approach to social interaction: he considered social life as a kind of theatre in which people assume different roles and act as if they are the directors of their life and of the impressions they awaken in others (a reminder of Pirandello).

In conclusion, symbolic interactionism is an orientation whose distinctive trait is the placement of social interaction and its interpretation from the viewpoint of those participating within it at the center of the analysis. From this perspective, what becomes central are the interpersonal processes through which individuals relate to each other according to their own way of thinking and that which they presume to be the other's, in order to choose the correct course of action to adhere to. At the same time, what is given prominence is the activity of symbolization undertaken by the individuals during the interaction and the development of the interpretive capacities of one's own and the other's experiences.

Sullivan's thinking was also influenced by the recent discoveries in the physical sciences, such as the theory of relativity of Einstein, who included the position of the observer in the description of reality, and the indeterminacy principle of Heisenberg, who underscored the reciprocal action between the object and the observer. These theories definitely undermined the concepts of objectivity and absolute truth (Hirsch, 1990). Basically, this means that what one sees is ultimately somehow dependent on who one is and from where and when one observes it. In other words, the observer is part of what is being observed. What emerges from this approach is the central concept of "participant observer", which synthesizes the Sullivanian approach to clinical investigation and the doctor-patient relationship.

Social psychology – another nascent discipline of this period – ultimately represented an essential reference point for theoreticians of interpersonalism and for Sullivan. The field theory of Kurt Lewin (1935) coincided with Sullivan's early ideas on interpersonal relationships. According to this theory, within a field of coexistent facts in their interdependence, the properties and the functions of each of them flow out of the relationships with all of the other present facts in the same field, within which no one thing can be understood and explained without the integration of the others. Sullivan expanded this vision of the field to include the evolutionary history of the person (Green, 1964).

The Neo-Freudian Culturalists

Freudian psychoanalysis was willingly accepted at the beginning of the twentieth century by American psychiatry, secure in its ability to take advantage of the correctional therapeutic system, in a vision that accentuated mechanicism, advancing the idea that psychic distress was due to the poor relationship between the internal structures of the psyche and then to a poor adaptation of the Ego to the situation (a genetic-structural direction). The person in this type of psychoanalysis was ahistorical. Thus, every connection between psychic distress and social experience, between personality and culture, was denied.

In this panorama are some important contributions that H. S. Sullivan, C. Thompson, K. Horney and E. Fromm made, ones which originate in statements theorized by Freud himself, such as the concept of "conflict" – between the individual and society, between nature and cultural demands. And this is why they in fact were initially considered "neo-Freudian culturalists".

For them, the suffering individual was no longer the consequence of a non-harmonic integration of their instinctual and evolutionary vicissitudes in the organization of the adult personality but reveals and is the reflection of a society in which interpersonal relationships, inadequate and pathogenic, do not consider people's need for sociality.

For Thompson and Sullivan, the need to remain tied to a reality – internal and environmental – in which the malaise has surfaced is a constant preoccupation.

With Karen Horney, a sort of apologia is also revealed for Roosevelt's American "New Deal" upon whose ideality she builds a model of moral tension in contrast with a human condition that she felt full of despair (the constant preoccupation with seeking the "true Self", the emphasis on self-analysis, etc. ...).

The culture, curiosity and intellectual freedom of these predecessors of ours meant they knew how to appropriate the anthropological research that had flourished between the two wars. The research convinced them that the determinism of the instincts was not enough to explain the actions and feelings of individuals.

The revision implemented regarding Freudian thought led to the elimination or the redefinition of the importance of the sexual drive, of the concept of the unconscious and of the process of repression.

The axis of the motivations of individuals shifted from the tyranny of instincts to the need for self-realization, independence and autonomy. With this adjustment of psychoanalysis towards a liberal and defiant morality, one would speak of self-realization and productivity, the building of the Self and identity, maturity and stability, optimism, strength of will and justifiable ambitions.

In conclusion, Sullivan was among the first and most distinguished advocates of the conjunction and reciprocal contamination between psychiatry and psychoanalysis at the end of the fifties.

Now we are ready to encounter H. S. Sullivan.

Chapter 2

Brief Biography of Harry Stack Sullivan

The Birth of the Group at the Forefront of the Story of Interpersonalism

Harry Stack Sullivan was born in Norwich, Chenango County, New York, on February 21 in 1892, into a poor Irish family that owned a farm in that county. According to the original project, Chenango County was supposed to become an important commercial hub thanks to the railway network intended to cross it, and for this reason many Irish emigrated there in search of fortune and financial stability. Unfortunately, the railroad was instead made to pass beneath it, and so the inhabitants remained completely cut off from any kind of profitable expansion, reduced as they were to moderate isolation and eventually exposed to poverty.

His biography demonstrates the close and direct connection between the social climate of the times and his psychological development. The isolation and loneliness he experienced meant that he never felt any attachment to the land on which he was raised (Conci, 2000).

I am pleased to begin with his life, thus allowing the reader to learn about this great man and his ideas from within, so to speak, through the most salient features that forged his identity. This will enable the reader to better understand his theory and feel more at ease with his principal concepts, no matter how new they may be or if never encountered before. To use his language, we will try to comprehend the way in which he arrived at the adult he became, what difficulties he encountered along the way and what were his chief interests and why.

Most of the facts regarding Sullivan's life come from a book written by his secretary and biographer, Helen Swick Perry (1982).

DOI: 10.4324/9781003512844-4

I will limit myself here to revealing the facts that mainly tie in with the theories he eventually developed.

So, let's return to his life.

His was not a happy childhood. Firstly, he was the only Sullivan son who managed to survive. Two other children, also born in winter, died shortly after they were born, their death caused by febrile seizures due to the intense cold.

It also seems that his mother suffered from a serious depression that kept her distant from her baby son of barely two years.

From Helen Swick Perry's biographical profile, it transpires that the child Harry lived very isolated. He was entrusted to grandmother Stack, whose strong Irish accent Sullivan fully inherited; Perry herself refers to the fact that he was hard to understand. It was indeed necessary to transcribe into decipherable English each of his lectures to create the texts we have at our disposal.

Clara Thompson (1949) describes Harry Stack Sullivan as a person who knew solitude at an extremely young age. His mother, who maintained that she had married beneath her, was a cold and morose woman who nurtured resentment for her family's humble situation. Harry received very little warmth from her. She was not interested in her son as a person, but she used him as a support to cultivate her own ambitions. Harry, however, felt that it was different with his father. His father was a timid and reserved person, but when Harry was an adult, they developed a true emotional bond. His only real childhood friends were the farm animals. He had no other companions. This was why he did not know how to become part of a group of peers once he started school, because he wasn't used to socializing. He was used to being alone.

Thompson maintained that these were the reasons why Sullivan was so motivated to understand loneliness and the suffering that may stem from it (Thompson, 1949).

The Stacks were less poor than the Sullivans. They owned a farm where Timothy Sullivan, his father, became a farmhand and later the owner, after having lost his job as a laborer. His mother, Ella, was not allowed to study, being the eldest daughter, and was therefore destined to care for her elderly parents, while the second daughter, Margaret, became a high school teacher and never married, perhaps because she never managed to find a suitor deemed worthy.

Harry's mother was convinced of having married a man much inferior in terms of social position, making do with him so as not to become a spinster, but her sister, having studied, seemed to have other aspirations. The fact remains that the Stack women assumed an air of superiority around the male sex, including Harry; however, they encouraged him to become impassioned with reading, knowledge, and study, something which accompanied him throughout his life and helped him endure the solitude and isolation that surrounded him until adolescence. In any case, it seems that he was emotionally very close to his father.

Sullivan would write unforgettable pages (1972) on the psychological condition of the only child, underscoring the difficult position in the family sphere, where that child is almost always too pampered and protected to the point of hindering a realistic evaluation of him/herself, often causing unpopularity with schoolmates and friends. This brings to mind the "special child" of John Fiscalini (1995a), regarding the etiology of narcissistic pathologies.

Sullivan was brought up in the Catholic faith but was not a practicing Catholic as an adult.

Every day the young Sullivan walked alone a distance of about six kilometers to the elementary school in the nearby village of Smyrna. His strong Irish accent exposed him to the ridicule of his schoolmates until his fortunate meeting around 1900 with Clarence Ballinger, who soon became his best friend. Clarence, also an only child, became his inseparable companion to and from school, picking him up from the farm in the caleche every morning and bringing him back the same way in the afternoon. In this way, Harry built up an intimacy with a person of the same sex, an "isophilic intimacy" about which I will speak when I touch upon the Sullivanian theory of development. Clarence, too, became a psychiatrist but never partnered with another person; he always lived alongside his mother even during his career.

Recognized at the Smyrna school for his acute intelligence, Harry benefitted from a scholarship that enabled him to go to college. He registered at Cornell University in 1908. We can imagine the excitement of our young man finally socializing among boys and girls of his own age.

Perhaps in order to attract the attention of the girl to whom he had taken a fancy, perhaps to be better received into the popular group in the college, Harry agreed to participate in a scheme to seize the money the students' parents sent on a monthly basis to the post office . While his accomplices were breaking into the post office at night, by forcibly shattering the lock, he stood guard outside. When the police arrived, everyone managed to escape except for our young student, who instead, in the wake of the incident, presumably had to grapple with a dissociative crisis. The actual diagnosis was "minor adolescent emotional disorder", but the fact remains that we only have information about Harry from about two and a half years later, when he had chosen to enroll in the faculty of medicine in Chicago.

In 1917 he graduated in Medicine and Surgery. He himself recounts that in 1915, while taking courses at the university, he studied psychoanalysis for the first time. His biography, however, reveals that he was essentially self-taught, thus, on the one hand, he had implicit gaps in his knowledge because he took this route, but on the other, he was freer of academic or theoretical prejudices of any type.

Immediately after graduation, during the First World War, he enlisted as a medical officer in the American army. He worked in a public institute of mental health and later became a Liaison Officer at St. Elizabeths Hospital in Washington D.C. This was a particularly important period in terms of his education and the sharpening of his sensitivity. It was in fact during these years, 1921 and 1922, that he met William Alanson White, who profoundly influenced him. White was the superintendent of St. Elizabeths and was a believer, along with Adolph Meyer, of the so-called New Psychiatry (see chapter 1), which looked at mental illness in a much less medicalized way and maintained that psychiatry had much to learn from the emerging sciences, the social sciences – anthropology and sociology – and should become integrated with them.

Ultimately, Sullivan was transferred to the Sheppard and Enoch Pratt Hospital in Towson, Maryland, where he also became the university chair in psychiatry. It was precisely at the Sheppard that he began to test another type of treatment for schizophrenia, especially in adolescent males, shortly becoming an authority in the field.

We can state that we owe to him the idea of what today is called, at least in Italy, "therapeutic communities". Since he found that the normal hospital procedures for schizophrenics were decidedly not therapeutic, he understood that it was necessary to approach this type of suffering by taking on full responsibility for the people afflicted with this illness. Aided by White, who entrusted an entire wing to him, Sullivan created a ward serving exclusively male schizophrenics (mostly adolescents). The patients were surrounded by assistants and nurses, carefully selected by Sullivan himself; they offered these boys a truly masculine model to identify with and to experience that "isophilic intimacy" that they needed.

Even though each patient had individual treatment, with Sullivan sometimes practicing hypnosis, the diversity of the environment of the ward, in which the patients were immersed twenty-four hours a day, was a particular focus. Sullivan was truly innovative in his staff selection process, and here we can point out his brilliant non-conformity: he didn't choose staff on the basis of qualifications but on the basis of their ability to empathize, and their non-conformity to social models. In this way, he thought that his ward could become a sort of school for life that could help nurture the personality of the patients in the context of the group.

It is interesting to note that Sullivan, who was never rich (nor did he ever seek to enrich himself), rented a big apartment to live close to his ward and offered keys to every member of his staff so that each of them could go there to relax when there was not enough time to go home. In this way, he fulfilled another aspect of fundamental therapeutic importance – he was able to facilitate meetings between assistants, doctors and nurses, who thus could discuss with each other the patients' state of improvement and build friendships and solidarity.

Thompson also wrote that he was not a very practical man. He basically had his head in the clouds, and he displayed many characteristics of the poet and artist, despite being a man of science. She went on to say that he was also a great lover of music, and perhaps this led him, along with his scientific investigatory prowess, to uncover so much meaning in the human voice (Thompson, 1949).

The Encounter with Clara Mabel Thompson, the Miracle Club and the Zodiac Group

It was in this period when a most important meeting in terms of the destiny of his theory took place: in 1923 he in fact met Clara Mabel Thompson, who became his inseparable life-long friend and who systematized his interpersonal theory of psychiatry, establishing interpersonal psychoanalysis – the adaptation of Sullivanian theory to psychoanalytic treatment.

In 1923, Clara was a particularly promising 30-year-old psychiatrist. She had been Adolph Meyer's right-hand woman at the Phipps Clinic, earning herself the jealousy and envy of all her colleagues, but she resigned and abandoned her mentor without hesitation because he frowned upon the analysis Clara had begun with a young doctor and gave her an ultimatum: either she dropped the analysis, or she was out. Clara did not hesitate to give up her excellent career prospects. She was willing to do anything to avoid yielding to this type of blackmail, which did not consider her personal pain and the need to expand her purely psychiatric horizons. She was also ill.

The meeting took place during a conference at the Phipps Clinic. She presented a paper on the suicide attempts of schizophrenics while she was suffering from a high fever due to a typhoid attack. Harry wished to make her acquaintance because of his interest in schizophrenia and because he was concerned about her illness (Green, 1964; Shapiro, 1993).

In 1930 Clara became the first president of the Washington-Baltimore Psychoanalytic Society, organized by Sullivan. In the same year, Sullivan was working in New York and teaching at Yale University with his anthropologist friend Edward Sapir. It was then that Clara started the Miracle Club, as the participants themselves called it: every week they gathered at Clara's house to discuss the most difficult cases that they were dealing with. Besides Clara, W. Silverberg and B.S. Robbins were also members of that small group of pioneers. Sullivan did not take part in these meetings because in that period he wasn't in Baltimore.

In 1931, these meetings had to end because Clara moved to Budapest to continue her analysis with Sandor Ferenczi, begun three years before, even if only during the summer.

The fact is Clara was not satisfied with the analysis she was engaging in from 1924 onwards with Joseph C. Thompson, a doctor with the same name – an analysis disapproved of by Adolph Meyer and which led to her dismissal from the Phipps Clinic because she refused to suspend it. Clara had then asked for Sullivan's advice. He recommended the Hungarian analyst because he was struck by the difference between Sandor Ferenczi and the European mainstream. Ferenczi was supposed to be on his way to New York in 1927 for some conferences at the New School for Research. Thus, Clara was able to meet him. She asked to be analyzed by him. The analysis ended in 1933, the year in which he died.

In 1933, with the help of Sapir and Harold D. Lasswell (political scientist and expert in the theory of communication, who formulated a theory of politics and propaganda based also on psychoanalytic criteria of Freudian origin and was also a member of what was later defined as the Chicago School of Social Sciences, in the tradition of Cooley, Mead, James, and Dewey), Sullivan founded the W. A. White Psychiatric Foundation, of which he was the first president, proposing an interdisciplinary approach. The psychiatrists who were educated here were also provided with a vast theoretical and sociocultural background. The orientation that came out of it was then always referred to as the Washington School of Psychiatry.

In 1938 Sullivan also founded the journal *Psychiatry*, which he edited up until his death in 1949.

Meanwhile, still in 1933, once Clara returned to New York, the group restarted and was now expanded to include some colleagues that had fled Nazi Europe. They were Karen Horney, Erich Fromm, and Frieda Fromm-Reichmann. The "Zodiac Group" was born, the name a fantasy of Sullivan's. Horney was represented by a water buffalo, Silverberg by a gazelle, Clara by a cat, and Sullivan by a horse, which symbolized the West Wind. According to one of the tales told to him by his grandmother, the West Wind was in fact one of his ancestors, portrayed as a horse running towards the rising sun to meet the future. This reveals something of Sullivan's sensitive nature with respect to his origins.

In the Zodiac Group there were also the Riochs and a few others. They got together every Monday evening for dinner at

Clara's house. In this period, Horney, who had emigrated to the USA not because she was Jewish but out of solidarity with her Jewish friends, taught and oversaw didactic analyses at the New York Psychoanalytic Institute, while Erich Fromm taught social psychology with an analytical inclination at the New School for Social Research in New York.

The Zodiac Club was heavily influenced by Sullivan's notion of psychiatry as a study of interpersonal dynamics. Psychiatry, he believed, should deal with the way in which each of us assumes a Self which values and loves, protects from doubts and criticisms, and which expands with praise, without taking much account of objectively observable behavior that includes contradictions and gross inconsistencies (Sullivan, 1938).

Lay Analysis and the Foundation of the William Alanson White Institute

In the meantime, a rupture had been forming in the New York Psychoanalytic Institute because of the age-old question of lay analysis, meaning analysis performed by non-doctors, like Fromm. Deeper motives concerned the attitude towards the social sciences, seen as a possible source of contamination of therapy and a loss of power on the part of psychiatry.

Karen Horney was practically forced to resign, and Clara Thompson followed her, out of solidarity but also indignation. The two of them, together with other colleagues, wrote a scathing letter denouncing dogmatism and power plays disguised as scientific controversies, which was later circulated among the members of the American Psychoanalytic Association (Green, 1964).

Unfortunately, this union and solidarity did not last long. In 1941, Clara, Horney, and Fromm were teaching at the newly established American Institute of Psychoanalysis. Horney and Fromm had a huge disagreement, probably due to rivalry and envy related to the continuously rising popularity of Fromm among the students. The fact is Fromm was divested of his role as a teaching analyst and was limited to a teaching role: basically, the same thing that a few months before had been done to Horney at the New York Psychoanalytic Institute. Clara's attitude, and that of her students and friends, had not changed, and therefore, the entire group, apart from Horney, who had voted against Fromm and against the possibility of non-doctors having didactic and analytical responsibilities, resigned from the American Institute of Psychoanalysis.

In 1943, this same group, obviously without Horney, who would soon establish her own institute, would establish the William Alanson White Institute of New York.

Still in 1941, Sullivan was hard at work for the U.S. Selective Service Commission, something that allowed him to develop his ideas in depth. In fact, this experience helped him to formulate the series of lectures that were then gathered posthumously in the 1954 book *The Psychiatric Interview*. His basic theories about personality are found in the 1956 book *Clinical Studies in Psychiatry*, which consists of the transcriptions of the lectures recorded by the staff and held at the famous Chestnut Lodge of Rockville, Maryland, between 1942 and 1946.

The Chestnut Lodge

It is worth mentioning a few words here about Chestnut Lodge, named by its founder, Ernest Bullard, after the approximately 125 chestnut trees that towered above the park. It was Bullard who turned it into a psychiatric hospital (first it was a luxury hotel, and then a sanatorium). The place boasted, among its directors, names like Frieda Fromm-Reichmann, Harold Searles, Alberta Szalita and Otto Will, besides being the place that inspired the famous novel by Joanne Greenberg, *I Never Promised You a Rose Garden* (1991), based on her therapeutic relationship with Frieda Fromm-Reichmann. In the novel, one can literally feel the distinctiveness of the type of countertransferal participation in the treatment.

Sullivan's lectures held at Chestnut Lodge are still remembered to this day, as he would comfortably sit in the armchair before the blazing fireplace of the library while lovingly caressing the Danish hound that snuggled up beside him (Perry, 1982).

Whoever is interested in obtaining further information on the history of Chestnut Lodge may consult among others the article on the subject by Ann-Louise Silver (1997), its last director.

Love in Sullivan's Life and His Death

After the Second World War, Sullivan participated in numerous international conferences. In 1948, he was very active in the foundation of the World Federation for Mental Health. He was a member of its Executive Board.

He met his death in a hotel in Paris, where he had gone for a conference.

Finally, a few words about love in his life. We know that he never married and that he was homosexual. We know for sure that around 1927 he met and had as a patient, if only for a short while, James Inscoe, a fifteen year old in the throes of dissociative crises found wandering the streets of New York. Jim, or Jimmie, as he came to be called, was adopted by Sullivan, who was twenty years older than him, and remained a friend for all his life. Perry tells us that Jimmie himself preferred to ignore the way in which they had met and refers to the fact that, during the time that Jimmie was typing Sullivan's manuscript about his own life, he objected to the reference of his being among his first patients, but Sullivan remained firm and did not want to make the change. In reality, it was true that Jimmie had never been a patient in the fullest sense of the word, but, Perry continues, it was also obvious that their relationship would never have begun if not for Sullivan's work. Unfortunately, Jimmie's family was not interested in him, and soon all the friends and especially the colleagues of Sullivan referred to Jimmie as "the man who came to stay" (Perry, 1982, p. 209), as Jimmie had already become important and a helpmate in the life of our pioneer.

There are only two documents in which we find a direct reference to the esteem and deep affection that Sullivan cultivated for him: the 1947 edition of *Conceptions of Modern Psychiatry* and his last will and testament, in which Sullivan left everything to him. The first text bears this dedication to Jimmie: "beloved foster son; without the support of whose affection, devotedness, patient forbearance, and good-natured self-sacrifice I would have accomplished little" (Perry, 1982, p. 209)

In the second, he refers to him as "my friend and ward in fact": "Said James Inscoe Sullivan has resided with me since the age of about fifteen years, and has been, in all senses, a son to me, and has my love and affection as much" (Perry, 1982, p. 210).

Until a few years ago, one could not speak about Sullivan's homosexuality at the White Institute if one wished to be certain about being able to finish one's training. It was better to keep silent. Today, fortunately, it is no longer like this, especially since colleagues like Jack Drescher and Mark J. Blechner have written extensively about it (Blechner, 2009).

Chapter 3

The Fundamental Concepts of Sullivan's Interpersonal Theory of Psychiatry

The Interpersonal Conception of Psychopathology

The theoretical point of view shared by many interpersonal analysts consists of the hypothesis of a universal conflict between the desire to stay within interiorized family configurations and the struggle for freedom, separation, and individuation.

> We shall assume that everyone is much more simply human than otherwise, and that anomalous interpersonal situations, insofar as they do not arise from differences in language or custom, are a function of differences in the relative maturity of the persons concerned ... I try to study the degrees and patterns of things which I assume to be ubiquitously (uniformly, commonly) human.
>
> (Sullivan, 1953, pp. 32–33)

The interpersonal conception of psychopathology makes reference to the need to adapt and be integrated into problematic family situations, as well as to the state of distress, linked to the emergence of those configurations, reflected in the attempt to save significant persons and not lose their love: these compromise adaptations are structured unconsciously and are continuously being actualized as a replica of past interiorized experiences.

The problems that the patient brings into the consulting room have more to do with the dynamic interiorized repetitions of the

DOI: 10.4324/9781003512844-5

past in the present than what happened in the past in and of itself (Hirsch, 1995).

The interpersonal tradition right from the beginning has therefore been characterized by its particular attention to the relationship, through the concepts of the interpersonal field and participant observation.

In this model, created mainly by a series of different approaches to theory and clinical practice, it is constantly emphasized that participating is inevitable, and embracing this point of view establishes a focus centered on the transference-countertransference dynamics.

Sullivan, even in his treatment of serious psychopathologies, remained constantly vigilant with respect to his own countertransference, never cultivating the illusion of being able to not be emotionally involved, considering it a definitive source of information in terms of the progress of the therapeutic process and the patient.

Basically, therapists are inevitably invaded and pervaded by their own feelings induced by the patient, feelings that give a specific coloring to each treatment, and which stimulate analysts to decodify the situation of which they are an integral part.

From this viewpoint, it appears clear how the interpersonal path has always valued the technical relevance of therapists as people, and consequently, the therapists' focus is always centered on countertransference. The clinicians' abilities chiefly depend on their subjective responses, their state of mind, their feelings, their fantasies, and their thoughts, considered in their totality as a fundamental technical framework for the identification and understanding of the patient's problem.

Sullivan's interpersonal theory is more useful than so many others from the therapeutic standpoint because it not only addresses what the individual is but also what the individual is experiencing in relation to his/her peers – experiences through which he/she suffers and grows.

For this individual, it is important to rediscover his/her interpersonal past through the eyes of the therapist, localize, with the therapist's help, the origins of his/her own way of thinking and feeling, and ultimately attain self-esteem.

Sullivan's Interpersonal Theory

Sullivan's interpersonal theory is based on the history of the significant relationships that each person has with other real beings. He sees the organization of the self as based upon the interactive patterns of these relationships, upon patterns characteristic of avoidance and the diminution of the distress developed via these relationships, and upon the degree to which the distress impedes the potential to remember, codify, process and associate the experience with other experiences.

As a result, Sullivan developed a model of the Self in which the concept of dissociation was central: dissociation represents the most important capacity of the human mind to protect its own stability (Bromberg, 1998).

Sullivan, in fact, maintains that most psychological difficulties arise from security measures put in place to protect one's stability and to avoid anxiety.

Even before the child learns to speak, certain attitudes of the people taking care of him/her, especially the mother, are transmitted through empathy. Subsequently, the parents' approval brings the child a sense of well-being, while their disapproval causes a sense of insecurity and anxiety/distress.

The latter represents for Sullivan a powerful force in the formation of the Self, interferes with observation, reduces the discriminatory capacities, and blocks the acquisition of awareness and comprehension. "Where there is anxiety, it tends to exclude the situation that provoked it from awareness" (Sullivan, 1947, p. 21).

The Fundamental Concepts of Sullivan's Thought

The fundamental concepts of Sullivan's thought can be summarized like this:

a   Needs
b   The concept of experience
c   The three modes of experience: prototaxic, parataxic, and syntactic
d   The three organizations of experience: the good me, the bad me, and the not me

e   The concept of anxiety
f   The Self
g   The concept of dynamism
h   The theory of development
i   The concept of parataxic distortion
j   The concept of personification
k   The concept of selective inattention
l   The concept of dissociation

The concepts of selective inattention and dissociation will be the subject of the second part of this treatise.

Now let us examine the above-mentioned points and define them conceptually.

a) Needs

Sullivan distinguishes between biological needs and needs of social relevance. The biological needs are basic, corresponding to the urgency of the instincts (hunger, thirst, the need for warmth, movement, sexuality, etc.). The needs of social relevance are instead created by the surrounding culture and centered around the need for security. The social needs do not necessarily derive, as in Freud, from the biological ones.

b) The Concept of Experience

The concept of experience concerns everything that is lived or felt. It is the internal component of the events in which a living organism participates as such (Sullivan, 1962).

c) The Three Modes of Experience: Prototaxic, Parataxic, and Syntaxic

The prototaxic experience takes place before the elements of such an experience can be attributed to a system of reference such as Ego awareness.

It is not yet differentiated according to a before and after, here and there, I and others, time and space, etc. ... It takes place in the pre-verbal phase of life, a phase in which experiences are inferred through zonal body perceptions, like the pleasure of sucking for that which concerns the oral zone, or possible displeasure drawn from sensations in the anal zone.

It is important to observe that Sullivan thought that the proto-taxic mode, like the parataxic, continues to be part of our way of establishing relations with others throughout the entire arc of our existence and pertains to situations we tend to minimize. Overall, we can consider prototaxic experience all those physiological reactions that we have with respect to our bodily needs. Often, we laugh about them, especially as adults, but we can say that they color our relationships with others. The earliest personifications, like those of the good breast and the bad breast, are formed in this type of experience, in which the basic element is the absence of a perception of limits. It has an enormous pathogenetic importance in the development of psychosis.

One can think of this modality as a *point de repère* of analytic listening.

In this first relational dimension, a primitive, prototaxic sensoriality is intermingled, and it involves and encompasses both the patient and the analyst. It is thus that the experience of being with the other begins to be formed (the Self with the other), through the mixing of primitive sensoriality, the vibration of the voice, the prosody that emanates from that which surrounds the other. With the term "sensorial", Sullivan is referring to all the channels through which one is aware of significant events, from the tactile organs to all types of sensitivity that have been developed to deal with one's own needs throughout the course of one's life. In *The Interpersonal Theory of Psychiatry* (1953), he gives the example of the luminous image, in which for each experience it is as if someone turned on a light bulb, and this constitutes a basic prototaxic experience. This mode of experience therefore con-stitutes a creative act, an artistic act as well as a unique one, in that the flow which enters ignites specific light bulbs and not others, which would be turned on if the "group of two" were made up of other people.

There is a phenomenological correspondence between the prototaxic mode and the subsymbolic experience of Wilma Bucci (2021), according to which crucial information regarding our bodily states streams into us in subsymbolic form, the principal way in which emotional communication occurs. In this sense, Theodor Reik's (1948) concept of "listening with the third ear" and Masud Khan's "hearing with the eyes" (1971) are largely based on subsymbolic communication, or, if we prefer, on the prototaxic mode, in interpersonal terms, all very current themes in the context of contemporary psychoanalysis, of studies on the mind/body relationship, in relation to early traumatic experiences.

The concept of the "agglutinated nucleus" of J. Bleger (1967) concerns something very similar. For Bleger, who expresses himself from the vantage point of object relations, the agglutinated nucleus is an archaic position, an extremely primitive level of mental functioning, which precedes the paranoid-schizoid and depressive positions and expresses a symbiotic constraint, a sort of "pact", as he defines it, between two individuals in which one uses the other as a depository of parts of the Self which cannot be integrated.

Around the eighth to ninth month of life, the child begins to use language, a moment which marks the beginning of the parataxic mode of experience. It is always relevant to childhood, and is characterized by a completely autistic, private use of verbal semantics; however, it is incompatible with the communicative process. There is already a differentiation of elements, but there is most of all a concurrence or conjunction of experience without any logical nexus. It is that which allows us to dream, to have reveries, and to daydream … .

At this point we should make some considerations about the Sullivanian theory of language. Sullivan maintained that humans communicate with others by means of gestures, therefore in a non-verbal way, and by means of language, in other words a verbal way. Nature has provided us with the ability to emit verbal sounds, but it is the culture that transforms these sounds into expressions rich with meaning through language. Growing up, we adapt our vocal sounds to those of our parents, who act as models. Sullivan made it clear that words do not transmit meanings but evoke them within the cognitive experience of those who become acculturated. Language can therefore be expressed via signs and symbols, each of which represents a pattern.

A sign is defined as a particular pattern in the experience of events which becomes differentiated by or through the general flux of experience (Sullivan, 1953). Signs evoke meanings, and we experience the meaning, not the sign, in an increasingly complex process: letters form words, words form sentences, and the sentences in and of themselves are intertwined more or less with the meanings they evoke. Signs and symbols are what make the human being capable of thought processes. When they symbolize events, we correlate them to other things, in the form of thought, words, and other aspects of our experience, which form more and more intricate webs of meaning.

The syntaxic experience refers to the communicative relationship; we are in the language stage.

More or less in the second year of life, around the eighteenth month, the child begins to live experience in a syntaxic mode, in which the understanding of the experience occurs for the child by means of consensual validation, or rather the capacity acquired through good enough experiences to be able to distinguish between what is fact and what is not, to formulate communicable knowledge, to make clear to others one's thought and presume that it is also theirs. As Sullivan says, syntaxic symbols are better represented by words that have been consensually validated, and consensus takes place when a child has learned the exact word for expressing a situation, not only the exact word of the common language but also what has assumed that meaning and not another for the mother and child, such as "da da da", which, for example, can mean father (dad).

Consensual validation is that type of interaction which should also characterize, according to Sullivan, the therapeutic situation (Conci, 2000, p. 463). We will see later on, especially in the chapter on Levenson, the importance that the mystification of meanings possesses in generating mental suffering and dysfunctionality.

d) The Three Organizations of Experience: The Good Me, the Bad Me, the Not Me

A brief mention now to the three organizations of experience: the good-me, the bad-me, the not-me. These concepts are fundamental to navigating the second part of this text.

The good-me and the bad-me stem from the experience relating to the mother's breast, whether it is satisfying or unsatisfying. Distress and "terrifying" experiences, the experience of an anxious mother, are relegated to the not-me, beyond consciousness, dissociated. The not-me is a primitive personification that gradually evolves and is organized via the parataxic mode and sometimes in the prototaxic mode. The partition between me (good and bad) and the not-me is the basic dissociative organization of the psyche.

Serious distress, abuse and interpersonal negligence in internalized relationships are dissociogenic.

Selective inattention is among the parataxic processes that avoid or minimize distress (see chapter 5).

e) The Concept of Anxiety

For Sullivan, anxiety can be understood only within the context of an interpersonal framework. For Freud, anxiety was associated with forceful instinctual needs, and a sense of security was linked to the regulation and control of these drives. For Sullivan, on the other hand, anxiety has a relational origin and is produced by the empathic bond with one's significant others. The Sullivanian concept of empathy pertains to the theorem of "reciprocal emotion", meaning that the integration into an interpersonal situation must be understood, as he sees it, as a reciprocal process in which the complementary needs are resolved or exacerbated, complementary ways of activity are developed or broken, and a prevision of satisfaction or frustration becomes possible.

> How is anxiety first generated? The tension of anxiety, when present in the mothering one, induces anxiety in the infant.
>
> (Sullivan, 1953, p. 41)

This is Sullivan's anxiety transmission theory. The mother's anxiety can thus remain in the child's implicit memory as a threat from which to protect him/herself, meaning that it becomes impossible for the child to integrate his/her own mental processes with the interactive processes in order to cope with a "blow to the head" type of experience, as Sullivan describes the experience of absolute absence and the dimension of emptiness that the child experiences due to the mother's anxiety.

The need for relief from anxiety is defined as the need for interpersonal security. In conclusion, anxiety is always an interpersonal event. Sullivan came increasingly to define anxiety in terms of self-evaluation:

> anxiety is a signal of danger to self-respect, to one's standing in the eyes of the significant persons present, even if they are only ideal figures from childhood (eidetic people); and this signal, other things being equal, leads to a change in the situation.
>
> (Sullivan, 1954, p. 218)

f) The Self

The Self according to Sullivan excludes everything that has remained dissociated under the impetus of anxiety. It doesn't contain all the evolutionary potentiality of human existence but only what develops in the desire to acquire social approbation and to avoid the loss of love; the adaptation mechanisms therefore arise as regulators of anxiety.

In 1931, he said that the self

> ...is built up of all the factors of experience that we have in which significant other people 'respond' to us. In other words, our self is made up of the reflections of our personality that we have encountered mirrored in those with whom we deal.
>
> (Sullivan, 1962, pp. 249–250)

The Self according to Sullivan is a security system: it is born out of the need to acquire security and tends to retain psychic equilibrium with defensive maneuvers like negation and avoidance of those aspects of reality that threaten the sense of security. Sullivan conceived of the Self as an organization of evasion and deviation, built to avoid anxiety and preserve one's own need for interpersonal security. This Self is often highly distorted; it is a fragile Self, which avoids serious distress and is only protected from dissociation and from those operations of security that are able to contain it and avert it. It is organized around dissociative gaps, through which anxiety returns to be felt as soon as the security procedures cannot prevent the painful experience.

If the dissociated, because anxiogenic, tends to become integrated, phenomena like acute panic, regression, fantasies, fascinated attention, stupor are produced ... and can reach serious fragmentation or schizophrenia. As Benedetti observes (1961), the important thing to note in this context is that this clinical nosology has a rigorously dynamic character: it does not pinpoint unhealthy entities as much as ways to be and protect oneself from distress.

The terms self, self-system and self-dynamism are used interchangeably by Sullivan, and occasionally he even referred to this identity concept as the Ego (Rychlak, 1973, p. 336).

g) The Concept of Dynamism

Dynamisms (not mechanisms) are ways in which energy systems are organized and channeled in the human organism. It is a non-static definition.

Generalized anxiety that emanates from the mother produces the dynamisms of the Ego (the Ego system); anxiety that arises out of the frustration of needs that have to be satisfied, and which comes from an exterior zone, and is therefore linked to the zones of the body, produces the specific dynamisms of that zone (zonal dynamism: energy surplus for that zone, which determines a need for exercise in that zone). For example: oral dynamism reproduces the anxiety caused by an energy surplus that goes beyond that of the biological function.

In conclusion, a dynamism is "a relatively enduring configuration of energy which manifests itself in characterizable processes in interpersonal relations", underscoring the human being's social side, and also "the relatively enduring pattern of energy transformations which recurrently characterize the organism in its duration as a living organism" (Sullivan, 1964, p. 35), where the biological and physiological side is highlighted.

h) The Theory of Development

The theory of development encompasses infancy, childhood, elementary school age, preadolescence, adolescence, late adolescence, adult age and old age. According to Benedetti, "... every age of development is limited in its capacity to provide new experiences, from distortions of character acquired in the previous age" (my translation, Benedetti, 1961, p. XIX). At the same time, it can however correct, remedy, and even cure certain previous gaps, when the preexisting distortion is not so serious as to have deeply injured it.

The newborn comes into the world in the parataxic mode of experience, possessing the major zones of interaction such as the oral acts relative to breathing, sucking, etc. This fixes the infant's attention on the maternal breast, which will later be personified as good or bad. In infancy, there are two ways to feel anxiety: either through a violent blow in a contact zone or through a lack of empathy with the mother.

In the infant, learning begins by means of primitive perceptions. In around the ninth month, the baby distinguishes between fear and anxiety and is sensitive to the changes in his/her level of anxiety, when he/she measures him/herself against parental expectations. The baby acquires, as well, the first rudimentary abilities of prevision.

During childhood, the child accepts surrendering some of his/her own personal needs to socialization and adapts to the requests of others, up until the maturation of the need for playmates. Sublimation becomes the dominant dynamism, reached through gradual identification, and the child plays at being the father and the mother. It is the age at which self-awareness grows and personifications of the Self quickly increase. We are around the second or third year of life and the first syntaxic experiences are beginning.

With elementary school age, the need for intimacy comes to the fore.

Thus, the school experience, which permits a comparison with the authority of one's own family, one's own lifestyle and that of others, can correct certain taboos, certain forms of neurotic dependency on one's own family (provided that the dependency has not reached such a degree as to render an effective criticism impossible) and permits social contact and an ability to compare and relativize.

(my translation, Benedetti, 1961, pp. XIX–XX)

The omissions to consider most serious are the earliest ones:

a very serious frustration in the first months alter personality, the structure of the first psychic acts, the 'core of the I', in such a catastrophic way that even in the future any situation will have difficulty generating a benefit.

(my translation, Benedetti, 1961)

Preadolescence and adolescence, which Freud, following exclusively the coordinates of sexual development, had defined as a "latency period", for Sullivan, represent a period of social presence, one of the most integrative of time periods, in which the search for the other becomes a constitutive element of one's own security and in which one experiences intimacy.

During the first school contacts, fundamental processes occur, such as competitive experiences, adaptations to a social system, the comparison between what happens in the family and cultural standards, and the relativization of the various types of authority – that is, the acquisition of a relative independence from infantile idealizations of that authority. In short, this is when character maturation first takes place.

In the period between 8 and a half and 12 years of age, the child enters preadolescence, the period that precedes sexual maturation and the interest in the opposite sex. This period is characterized by the manifestation of the need for an "isophilic intimacy", meaning the need for intimacy with another of the same sex, "the playmate": this partnership succeeds competition and compromise. Affection in a mature sense begins, where the satisfaction and security of the other become as important as one's own (Buber, 1984). All the autistic ideas and fantastic personifications of oneself and others can now be tested via the experience of the best friend.

Adolescence is characterized by the need for gratification of desire, including genital desire. Here the problems arise from the confusion over the fact that "erotic" love is not necessarily "philic" as well.

Sullivan stated that one enters late adolescence when one discovers which genital practices one likes and how to adapt them to the rest of one's life. In general, the mature person has learned how to live in a satisfying enough way. It is certainly essential that the mature personality reflects a need for intimacy and connection with at least one person, but preferably more than one. For Sullivan, only the pre-adolescent and adolescent have developed the capacity to love. Here he provides one of the most beautiful definitions: "When we love someone, we care more about the other person's satisfactions and security then we do about our own" (Sullivan, 1940, pp. 42–43)

All those who, irrespective of chronological age, have not reached this maturity cannot feel love; nonetheless, under the effect of social pressure, they do their best to conform and scrupulously execute the gestures of being in love. Since they have a great need to feel secure, they do their best to make their performance very convincing, not only for others but also for themselves. Their emotional demonstrations, sometimes knowingly fraudulent, but often carried out in good faith, can be extravagant and completely incompatible with reality. (Sullivan, 1940)

The sense of loneliness in preadolescence and adolescence is an experience that is the result of failed integration. It is in the fluctuation between anxiety and loneliness that many mental disorders are formed. Loneliness that is caused by the untenability of anxiety impels one towards forms of defective integration.

Sullivan sees the stages of development primarily within the social process, of which the development of body zones is an integral but not dominant part.

i) The Concept of Parataxic Distortion

The concept of parataxic distortion embraces within itself the concepts of transference and projection, already formulated by

Freud. Parataxic distortion in an interpersonal situation occurs whenever at least one of the two participants reacts to a personification, namely to an image of the other, one which exists only in their own fantasy – a sort of human representation pre-formed from past experiences, one which is evoked by certain real aspects of the other.

j) The Concept of Personification

Two categories of people are present, more or less consciously, in everyone's life: those who are real and those who are imaginary, or "covered", or "eidetic", emanating from real experiences and formed at the point of encounter of the individual character with the world which receives them. They are "fantastic personifications" which have a certain connection to the social world but represent an elaboration of it different from simple memory insofar as they are detached from reality (Benedetti, 1961, p. XIII) (for example: qualities inherent in distinctive facts can be merged into a single figure that synthesizes and exaggerates them).

Eidetic figures are not able to be revealed through simple introspection but through a comparative examination of different mental acts – in other words, by inference. These are set apart from real partners due to their static rigidity. They are the "rush of experiences" that form character. However, they, too, grow and are transformed by the evolution of all the other life experiences as well as by the possible influences of "corrective experiences", like psychotherapy, in which there is an "an infusion little by little" of the sense of reality through the "consensual validation" of what pertains to the internal world and what pertains to reality.

We must not omit a final concept concerning the illusion of personal individuality. In his own words:

> For all I know every human being has as many personalities as he has interpersonal relations; And as a great many of our interpersonal relations are actual operations with imaginary people – that is, in no sense materially embodied people – and as they may have the same or greater validity and importance in life as have our operations with many materially-embodied

people like the clerks in the corner store, you can see that even though 'the illusion of personal individuality' sounds quite lunatic when first heard, there is at least food for thought in it.

(Sullivan, 1964, p. 221)

Before going on to the treatment of dissociation, it is important to emphasize that the overview just provided of the fundamental concepts of Sullivanian theory is absolutely to be considered fragmentary. I have tried to highlight only those concepts that can be useful for an in-depth study of the concept of dissociation and its clinical use, omitting many of his ideas and many aspects of his theory, and so I recommend to those interested in these to undertake a direct reading of Sullivan's texts themselves.

Certainly, he profoundly influenced the etiopathogenetic cognition of schizophrenia, and its treatment, showing how this disorder had roots in the interpersonal history of the patient. With this he did not mean to deny the hereditary or biological component of schizophrenia but to highlight the importance of relational events with significant figures.

Chapter 4

From Sullivan's Interpersonal Theory of Psychiatry to Interpersonal Psychoanalysis through Clara Mabel Thompson

It is incumbent upon me to again emphasize in this chapter how psychological theories derive in a significant measure from the subjective interests of their creators. I will not be able to expand as much as I would like to on the psycho-biographical aspects of Clara Mabel Thompson. I will only make a few indications to show where her personality lies within them.

The role of connector and filter that Clara Thompson has played and embodied in the evolution of the theory and practice of psychoanalysis is often undervalued.

I believe that this has happened for several reasons but mostly because of the characteristics of the personality of Thompson herself, who, from her biography and from those who have passed on to us their memories of her, appears rather solitary and reserved.

Clara M. Thompson's Life

Clara Thompson graduated in psychiatry in 1920. Almost immediately after graduation she worked at the Johns Hopkins Institute and simultaneously at the New York Infirmary for Women and Children. At the end of the year, she returned to Johns Hopkins and began an internship in Psychiatry at the Phipps Clinic with Adolf Meyer. It was precisely during the second year of this internship, in which she became the right arm of Meyer, earning the envy and rivalry of her colleagues, that she met Sullivan, during a conference on adolescent suicide at the Phipps Clinic

DOI: 10.4324/9781003512844-6

(Thompson, 1949). Their synergy, which would bring inter-personal thought to life, emerged from this encounter.

She dealt with the conceptual issues of the interpersonal para-digm with a view to establishing a theory and a practice in her first book: *Psychoanalysis: Evolution and Development* (1951). And thus Sullivan's interpersonal theory of psychiatry became inter-personal psychoanalysis.

We must highlight the inevitable influence that the ideas of Sandor Ferenczi had on Thompson in the deliberation and reali-zation of this task, following her analytical experience with him, upon the recommendation of Sullivan, in Budapest from 1928 to 1933 (see chapter 2).

The fundamental concepts upon which Thompson lays down the basis of a psychoanalytic theory established on Sullivan's model of interpersonal psychiatry are:

a) Transference
b) Transference and character structure
c) The use of transference in psychoanalysis
d) Countertransference
e) Parataxic distortion
f) Therapy

a) Transference

For Thompson, transference consists entirely of irrational atti-tudes in relation to another person.

She speaks of it as an often-abused concept: one must never forget that even the most neurotic or even psychotic of patients can come to trust in their own analyst and love them not only via transference but also because the analyst is interested in the patient and truly helps that patient.

One should also always remember that the patient is not alto-gether lacking in judgment. Transference is therefore everything that the patient irrationally transfers onto the analyst, or that he/she exaggerates or minimizes, starting with the analyst's activity: the real personality of the analyst thus assumes a fundamental importance.

This concept of transference without a doubt is derived from Ferenczi's thought. Ferenczi was convinced that very young children perceive and react to their parents' personality. This occurs as well in the relationship that is created in analysis. Therefore, patients not only act through transference but they react to the true personality of the analyst. Thompson concludes with one of the fundamental nuclei of interpersonal theory: the analyst's personality is the instrument of healing.

b)   Transference and Character Structure

For Freud, transference originates in the child's attitude towards his/her parents during the oedipal complex. For Thompson, influenced by Ferenczi's thinking, character structure is formed instead beginning with the relationship with the mother figure, through which a system of modalities of adaptation to individuals, similar to the mother, is developed.

Then there is a second person, the father or a brother or another figure, and the child soon learns that he/she must modify his/her way of reacting if he/she wishes to also please them.

Even after the period of the oedipal complex, other significant personalities can influence the modalities of behavior, or rather various models of behavior are formed in one person alone, all as a reaction to the significant figures of the past.

Some figures may stand in complete contradiction to one another, and the earliest are the strongest. This expresses the conceptualization of the so-called multiplicity of the Self – that is, the combination of the various Selves, which everyone is continuously building. As Bromberg has observed (1998, 2006), the problem for the individual becomes the ability to simultaneously negotiate continuity and change, the essential ingredients for a sense of being oneself, which is indispensable to mental health. The analytical relationship for Bromberg has this precise clinical task, to help the patient recover the capacity of being in the spaces of his/her personality, in its multiplicity, in being one among many.

Character structure is therefore understood by Thompson (1964) as an ensemble of defensive reactions, originating from transference and reinforced by repeated life experiences. We can't resolve it by simply referring it to the originating situation, because subsequent experiences, which also include neurotic aims, have become part of its structure. The compulsion to repeat is not only a forced reliving of the past guided by the death drive but a re-creating of analogous interpersonal situations.

All of this may be read in Sullivanian terminology as "parataxic distortion".

c) The Use of Transference in Psychoanalysis

The more the patient observes their own behavior within themself, the more they become aware of its origin, and they ultimately realize that they are dominated by the fear of disapproval.

They question the why of so much fear, and then a chain of memories – some from childhood, and some not – provides them with the proof of the origin of this fear and of its subsequent development.

Psychoanalytic theory consists of a series of such discoveries relative to personality. Every discovery is followed by a modification of personality with a view to healing. The dynamic use of transference as a therapeutic instrument therefore leads to lasting personality changes.

d) Countertransference

From the beginning of his work with patients, Freud realized that the presence of the analyst, within the therapeutic relationship, brings with it elements that make the situation unclear and nonobvious, aspects to somehow keep under control.

His recommendation, so as not to run into disagreeable situations, is to stay as anonymous as possible and not forge any type of social relationship with patients.

What was advised was a position in which the analyst is seated behind the patients, in order to prevent them from reading the expressions that appear on the therapist's face, and it is recommended that no personal element be revealed during the treatment. Herein lies so-called neutrality.

Despite this, some aspects, starting with the analyst's sex, his/her style of dressing, the objects contained in the consulting room, and information gathered from other sources, cannot be avoided. Thus is born the necessity of delving more deeply into these phenomena as a whole.

At the beginning of the twenties, Freud clarified how some personal difficulties of the analyst could bring about emotional entanglements that would thwart the success of the treatment. This has come to be called countertransference. Personal analysis was advised to "cure" it.

Ferenczi was one of the first to realize that what is needed is a much longer and deeper process than the one reserved for patients so that the analyst may be able to subsequently do a good job.

Proceeding from the stimuli issuing from Ferenczi's work, Sullivan, Thompson and Fromm- Reichmann encourage the idea of greater participation on the part of the therapist in the analytic situation and awareness of how a greater straightforwardness may be necessary within the therapeutic relationship, which also implies the admission of possible errors committed.

From this point forward, Thompson's contribution is fundamental and represents the basis for the majority of future work on the subject (see chapter 7).

She distinguishes the analyst's normal reactions, like becoming annoyed because the patient never wants to go to the end of the session, from the reactions based on the analyst's own problems, such as becoming annoyed due to personal prejudice, for which it becomes essential that the analyst analyzes him/herself. Countertransference thus is defined as the transferring of the irrational aspects of the analyst's personality in the relationship with the patient (Thompson, 1964).

The analyst should be as free as possible of anxieties and defensive attitudes, but being a human being, what is *truly* important is that he/she is aware of his/her own difficulties and that he/she is capable of speaking about them with the patient, in case the analyst becomes aware that these difficulties are influencing the therapeutic situation in some way.

This candidness often leads to greater collaboration on the part of the patient.

The most difficult of the problems related to counter-transference is tied to the overcoming of what has remained unresolved in the analyst's defensive system. He/she could there-fore have difficulty in facing hostility and for this reason may not be aware of the patient's hostility, or if he/she has low self-esteem, he/she would struggle to indicate the patient's disparaging atti-tudes. And finally, if the analyst possessed a trace of a sadistic or authoritarian attitude, he/she could intimidate the patient, who might become compliant due to being frightened.

The important thing is to continue to try to understand what is happening between us and the patient, all the while staying humble, in order to be able to learn something new about our-selves – always.

An important tool available to therapists is supervision, the main function of which is having a wider vantage point, an over-view which eludes the participants and is fundamental for over-coming countertransferential difficulties.

Thompson highlights the importance of group discussion (today we could say intervision) for the evolution of her clinical work and thought. The group represents a place where every participant can give suggestions for reflection on problematical points regarding clinical situations.

The analyst's personality, moreover, is not only a negative aspect but is the heart, the essence of analysis. Without its pecu-liarities, a transformative encounter between two people would not be possible. It is the infinite personal nuances that bring about the possibility of working with countless people that request help.

For Thompson, in order to be able to understand and not fall victim to countertransferential elements, it is just as important to pay attention to the non-verbal and to take into consideration the function of the analyst's values, which influence his/her way of tackling problems and can prove difficult for the patient to accept.

If Freud asks the analyst to be a morally honest person, Thompson hopes that he/she knows how to confront his/her own blind spots.

The step has been taken. The groundwork has been con-solidated. The complexity of the analytical situation is beginning to be considered in all its ramifications, with seriousness, humility, and determination.

e) Parataxic Distortion

Parataxic distortion contains the two Freudian concepts of transference and character structure.

Each individual when entering a relationship with another can see things in that other that do not exist within him/herself and then he/she reacts to these things.

Parataxic distortion thus comprises all those illusory attributes created by the previous life experiences of the subject.

The term *parataxic* indicates the infant's way of thinking, feeling, or acting before the child feels the need to communicate with others in a specific way. Thus, a word may have a very personalized meaning depending on what the child associates with it. This type of thinking remains active to some extent in all of us for all of life.

The concept of parataxic distortion is developed by Sullivan, who notices how the relationship between two people always includes some "fantastic personifications", characteristics taken from important people of the past attributed to people to whom we are relating in the present. In contrast with Freud's transference, Sullivan does not see the origin of "parataxic distortion" only within the oedipal situation; he wished to highlight its non-sexual origin and include in the term the character defenses.

This means that for Sullivan this takes place in all interpersonal relationships, not only in analysis. One of the most important goals of therapy is that of making the patient aware of what is happening between him-/herself and others based on distorted identifications. In this context, the analytic situation is only a valid example.

Therefore, in the final analysis, parataxic distortion is every attitude towards another person based on a fantasy or the identification of oneself with other significant figures.

One way to distinguish what is real or parataxic in the thoughts about and feelings for another person is "consensual validation" – that is, a comparison of one's own evaluation with those of others. In this way, many ideas can be corrected by getting as close as possible to an approximation of truth.

f)   Therapy

Therapy lies in gradually making clear to the patient what he/she does *to* other people and *with* other people, since he/she sees them in a distorted way.

However, it is not enough to understand the history of the development of his/her distortions: one must also understand that the patient clearly sees what function they have in the present and how they meet his /her needs.

In conclusion, the concept of parataxic distortion certainly involves the Freudian concepts of transference and character structure, but the original theory is different from it: Sullivan always sees personality from the perspective of intercommunication with other personalities.

Section II

Chapter 5

Dissociation

Similarities and Differences Between the Concept of Splitting and that of Dissociation

If you like the films of Quentin Tarantino or Paolo Sorrentino, or if you like novels like *Catcher in the Rye* by Salinger, or if you have been won over by Anatole Frances's description of poor brother Paphnuce in the throes of his – dissociated – yearnings for Thais, in the eponymous novel, or you are passionate about the lyrics of many rap and/or contemporary pop songs, you will find this chapter especially crucial and illuminating. The list I have provided could be expanded upon with so many other names, as well as other areas of interest, but for obvious reasons of space, I have limited myself to a few examples. I leave to the readers the pleasure of making their own connections with their life experience, by engaging with the concept of dissociation from the viewpoint of interpersonal psychoanalysis.

Selective Inattention and Dissociative Processes

Let us begin by saying that among the parataxic processes that avoid or minimize distress there is selective inattention. This process maintains dissociation by means of the conscious control of the events that engulf us.

In selective inattention, the person is simply not aware of certain aspects of his/her own life. He/she eliminates them and neither sees nor perceives them. Sullivan wondered how it is possible that people have painful and terrible experiences, as if they are pounding their head against a stone wall, even more than once a day, and do not learn from them. He deduced from this that there is only one

DOI: 10.4324/9781003512844-8

possible explanation, what he would call *selective inattention*: a universal human characteristic which allows one to stay the same in large measure despite even deeply painful experiences, by keeping one's attention on something else.

Selective inattention is in fact selective. In other words, there is a constant vigilance in *not* noticing certain things. The aspects of life that are selectively disregarded must have been in some way connected to or circumscribed as areas of grave danger. Selective inattention allows one to avoid having to change oneself as a result of experiences that we have with others. But the most important thing of all is that it allows one to not feel any anxiety, angst or agitation of any kind.

Concentration is a part of such a process. Practically speaking, when we must do something that involves the use of the analytic/synthetic apparatus made available to us by biology, we are capable, but only *for a short time*, of more or less focusing this apparatus on an extremely small situation. If prolonged, this extremely intense concentration could be damaging for the psyche.

Therefore, selective inattention is the capacity to separate attention from consciousness, to "restrict" or "suspend" awareness. We all possess this ability.

Let us recall how for Sullivan nothing is more important than the preservation of a sense of security and self-esteem. Thus, we know that, by means of selective inattention, consciousness may receive the relevant elements and exclude the irrelevant ones, which, however, will always be present in some other place.

In selective inattention, the event becomes detached from its context; *it becomes divested of importance. Restricting consciousness*, therefore, and *limiting memory* allow one to remember only useful experiences and avoid at the same time the awareness of those irrelevant or disturbing ones.

What is of interest to therapists concerns those moments when one does not pay attention to what is relevant. Therefore, selective inattention occurs in two types of situations:

1 When one is engaged in a very difficult activity in which one cannot get distracted (as in the example of target shooting).
2 When the situation concerns the stability of the Ego system.

Selective inattention is no use in suppressing needs (as in sublimation) but *only* in preserving security, which is the task of the Ego.

We can say then that we use selective inattention for two reasons:

1   To concentrate to the maximum extent of human abilities on a particularly difficult task.
2   To avoid anxiety.

The misperception of a situation is not maladaptive until the contents of that experience have been literally dissociated from the Ego system.

Within this framework, *dissociation* means that things have become *entirely cut off* from identification with the self. Sullivan makes no distinction between selective inattention and dissociation, as he has a vision of the entire process on a continuum.

Dissociative dynamism is therefore always active and – an apparent contradiction – always vigilant. It is a continuous state of being alert, and when something in life is about to reveal dissociative content, then the self-system demonstrates its capacity to change the topic of conversation, by shifting the nucleus of the discourse, or simply by dismissing the thing as "annoying". These are the defensive maneuvers that Sullivan calls substitute processes, because they replace a healthier process in which the person would compare and contrast his not-me behaviors. This is not different in the child nor in the adult; indeed, the adult, who is more sophisticated, can "cover up" with better success than the child, who has not yet reached a sense of secure identity. (I advise a reading of the two examples that Sullivan offers on the subject in *Clinical Studies*, 1956).

The Concept of Dissociation

In a general sense, dissociation refers to the separation of mental and experiential contents that would normally be connected. The word dissociation is laden with multiple meanings and refers to many kinds of phenomena, processes, and conditions.

(Howell, 2005, p. 18)

It is both adaptive and maladaptive, both cause and effect (Spiegel, 1990; Tarnopolsky, 2003). "Dissociation is often psychologically defensive, protecting against painful affects and memories" (Tarnopolsky, 2003), but it can often be the organism's automatic response to imminent danger.

Those physical events such as stepping outside of oneself (being spaced out), psychic numbness, and even the experience of floating above one's own body, as in some far eastern techniques, are also to be included in dissociative phenomena.

There exist many views of the etiology and the nature of dissociation. "These views converge around the idea that dissociation represents a failure of integration of ideas, information, affects, and experience" (Putnam, 1997, p. 19). All these different meanings potentially create a conceptual confusion, to the point where dissociation loses its precise meaning, as has occurred in the case of other concepts (just think for example of the concept of the Self, of identity, of the unconscious, etc. ...).

Lastly, dissociation can be conceived as a taxonomic fact, or as existent on a continuum which describes each one of us, although in varying degrees. In the taxonomic model, we refer to dissociation classified through symptoms, as for instance in dissociative disorders, while the other model, the dimensional model, places it on a continuum which from adaptive, normative dissociation reaches to the extremes of pathological dissociation. Both models are supported by clinical evidence, but the significant difference between the two positions has created confusion and conceptual disorientation. In this text, we will use this term according to the continuum model.

The Continuum from Mental Health to Psychopathology

It is important to clarify that dissociating is not necessarily the obvious proof of a traumatic history or that we are dealing with psychopathology.

If we place it along a continuum, we see that at the healthy extreme of this continuum there are dissociative experiences that are normative – that intensify and enhance pleasure, joy and affectivity in life.

A first example is absorption, or rather intense concentration – being completely absorbed by something. It presents itself as the ability to allow oneself to be transported into a focus of attention so confined, to allow oneself to be immersed in an experience so crucial that the context finally loses its contours – a type of concentration that one has when one becomes immersed in a book or a film, or while we are driving, or when meditating, or experiencing reverie, like in positive trance experiences, which involve the loss of self-reflective consciousness.

Another dissociative phenomenon, always at the healthy extreme of the continuum, is the so-called highway hypnosis – that is, the phenomenon that occurs when we are driving a well-known route and find ourselves at our destination without having any awareness of what happened along the way.

To better understand when dissociation is adaptive and when it is pathological, one can think about how the process occurs by virtue of will, as in meditation.

Putnam's research (1997) led him to state that there are aspects of dissociative ability linked to age: the capacity to dissociate is very great in childhood and gradually decreases with age, except for the period of adolescence. A significant capacity to dissociate permeates during adulthood only in the presence of traumatic abuse, even if the individuals who undergo abuses in adulthood but did not present traumas during childhood show that they use dissociation but not in an extensive way (Howell, 2005, p. 18).

However, dissociation can have defensive elements. This occurs when a person has found dissociation in order to endure traumatic situations. They willingly and deliberately enter into a state of trance or absorption, "becoming lost in the wallpaper, or mentally going into a mousehole in the wall" (Howell, 2005, p. 20).

Dissociation According to the Interpersonal Model

Now let's return to Sullivan's thought and his conceptualizations.

Sullivan has described how some types of experiences can become dissociated by becoming part of the not-me (chapter 3). Herein lies, for Sullivan, the interpersonal genesis of dissociation. It emerges out of unbearable angst felt in the interactions with caregivers, including the extreme disapproval of parents. In these cases, the experience remains unformulated, and therefore dissociated.

Hence, dissociation refers to *the unconscious avoidance of formulating aspects of the experience into meaningful constructs.* And lastly, the culture itself can be dissociogenic and discontinuous, to the extent that even the experiences of the self are marked by discontinuity.

As we have seen, the interpersonal school has utilized from the beginning, with the philosophy of H. S. Sullivan, its founder, the concept of dissociation in order to create its own theory of the mind and its own theory of technique.

I don't know if it would be accurate to say that Sullivan was one of the first to abandon the perplexity of the term "split", which like "spaltung" in German refers, in that era, to both the splitting, a noun dear to the *psychoanalytic* environment within which it assumed more and more variegated shadings of meaning over time in relation to the *structures*, and to dissociation, a term forever used by *psychiatry* in its dealing with *functions*, namely the processes or mental activities or even more or less complex sets of activities or processes, like perception, memory, thought, etc. It is certain that Sullivan, from the beginning, exclusively and directly used the term "dissociation" for referring to *the central modality of the structure of the self.*

Sullivan developed his theory of anxiety, trauma, and dissociation by basing it on interpersonal interaction and elaborated a model of the Self in which the concept of dissociation was central.

As Philip Bromberg observes (1998), Sullivan's theory is essentially a theory of the dissociative organization of the self in response to trauma. In this way, Sullivan restores to psychoanalytic thought the centrality of the phenomenon of dissociation, defining it as the most important ability of the human mind to protect its own stability.

It seems to me that a significant and substantial peculiarity of the concept of dissociation in interpersonal theory is emerging here: dissociation is a normal reaction to a trauma. Anyone can dissociate if placed before an intolerable catastrophe which goes beyond one's capacity for coping, and this makes us better able to understand dissociative character disorder – the so-called multiple personality – in those who must learn to dissociate as a habitual reaction to traumas they are undergoing.

The advantages of dissociation in unbearable conditions are obvious: one becomes detached from pain, from horror and from terror. Of course, the price to pay is high because there is the risk that this defense will also work automatically when survival is not really at risk and when from its own global functioning it would be possible to extract more discriminating adaptations to the threatening situation, transforming the identity of the person using it.

Differences Between Splitting and Dissociation

It is interesting to note that in the encyclopedia of psychoanalysis of Laplanche and Pontalis (1974) the word dissociation simply does not appear. This demonstrates what I said at the beginning of this chapter: that the term dissociation was not considered a term characteristic of psychoanalytic language.

With respect to splitting, these two authoritative authors describe a splitting of the Ego (Freud) and a splitting of the object (Klein). With splitting of the Ego (*Ichspaltung*), Freud designates a phenomenon observed mostly in fetishism and psychosis: the coexistence within the Ego of two psychic attitudes towards external reality in opposition to an instinctual need; one takes account of reality, the other denies it and replaces it with a product of desire. These two attitudes persist side by side without influencing each other. The splitting of the object with Melanie Klein is defined as the most primitive defense against anxiety and is mostly active in the paranoid-schizoid position.

Let us now look at the rather subtle but nevertheless existing difference between the concept of "negation" and that of "denial".

The term negation (*verneinung, negazione, negaciòn, (de)nègation, negacao*) is defined by Laplanche and Pontalis (1974) as a process by which the subject, although formulating one of his/her previously repressed desires, thoughts or feelings, continues to defend him/herself from it, by denying that it belongs to him/her (Laplanche and Pontalis, 1974).

In German, *verneinung* designates both *negation* in a logical or grammatical sense and *denial* in the psychological sense (in other words, the rejection of a statement a person has articulated, or that has been attributed to them, along these lines: no, I did not say that; I did not think that). *Verleugnen* is close to *verneinen* in this second sense: disavowal, rejection, repudiation, denial.

In Italian, one distinguishes between *negazione* (negation) in the logical and grammatical sense and *smentita* or *diniego* (denial), which imply objection or rejection; the clear negation of the perception of a fact that is imposed in the external world (Laplanche and Pontalis, 1974).

Treccani, the encyclopedia of the Italian language, defines *negazione* as:

> the act of negating, and the expression with which it is negated (the opposite of affirmation). It can be resolute (disavowal), timid, or stubborn. In psychoanalysis: a defense mechanism by means of which the subject goes against the conscious perception of forbidden thoughts or desires, denying that these can be attributed to him.
>
> (Treccani, 1986, p. 382)

It seems important to immediately point out that here it is evident that negation implies repression, as it occurs in splitting.

If, therefore, disavowal of reality is a means of defense, which consists of a clear-cut rejection on the part of the subject in the recognition of the reality of a traumatizing perception, negation is instead a less explicit, less resolute rejection. In conclusion, one can think of splitting as a defensive modality for reducing distress and maintaining self-esteem if subjected to ambiguous or threatening experiences (of the good/bad kind). It uses negation.

Let us recall now the concept of the vertical split (Kohut, 1971), according to which trauma can create a personality split which separates an entire segment of the psyche from that which includes the central Self, and which is manifested by an alternating of states of grandiosity that deny the frustrated need of approval, with states in which feelings of emptiness and low self-esteem predominate. Horizontal splitting is defined, on the other hand, as a barrier of repression that is manifested by the patient's emotional aloofness and his/her insistence on maintaining distance from objects from which he/she could desire narcissistic support.

Thus, splitting is produced at a much deeper level by repression, and at a more superficial level by negation. It uses *repression* (in repression there is no amnesia; one can bring to mind what has been repressed) and *negation*. Basically, vertical splitting is the way in which Kohut manages to formulate the concept of dissociation (Albasi, 2006). It is a structural, chronic and specific change, associated with the mechanism of *denial*.

Let us look at the similarities between Kohut's concept of vertical splitting and that of dissociation: both concepts refer to a reaction to trauma, in which there is total detachment and in which denial is used.

Vertical splitting originates when one's needs seem to represent a threat to the relationships of attachment because they are in opposition to the needs of the parental figures. In this case, we can speak of an organization of a not-me type of experience, in other words – a dissociative one. It involves an unconscious projective identification with those aspects of the psyches of the parents that do not tolerate the needs of the child, for whom these needs end up in the bad-me, and they remain felt as unsatisfied and thwarted, while in the not-me the parental inadequacies converge, or rather the rejecting or abusive or intolerant other forcefully enters into the psyche and from then on can act undisturbed because dissociated.

The clinical forms most characteristic of vertical splitting are behavior disorders, in particular the dependency behaviors – addiction disorders – eating disorders, perversions, and criminal activities.

In conclusion, the term splitting is not adopted in the interpersonal mode, for reasons I have already fully covered. I maintain, however, that the use of the term dissociation within this model is in its conceptual meaning very close to that of vertical splitting.

As a final comment, I would like to point out the difference between dissociation in the Sullivanian model and dissociation in Janet (1889): in Sullivan it is motivated by a person's need to not know, whereas for Janet it was more a consequence of a psychic oppression due to a powerful stress, to a trauma. Sullivan's not-me instead organizes the person's experience, and it is developed whenever the person is engulfed by intense angst.

Chapter 6

The Interpersonal Field

Interpersonal Field and
Intersubjective Field: Two Different
Concepts?

Field theory is based on Maxwell's electromagnetic field model
(1860–1870) in physics. Every person is immersed in a field of
forces that act simultaneously, pushing him/her in different direc-
tions. The field is a representation of the situation in a given
moment and is defined as a totality of coexistent facts in their
interdependence (Hirsch, 1998).

For Kurt Lewin (1951) a group is a dynamic totality of members in close interdependence, in which a change of an element
affects all the other components.

Field Theory in Sullivan

The field concept in Sullivan reflects Lewin's theory (1935),
according to which the forces that govern behavior can be understood only in the light of the entire psychological situation – that
is, by studying the subject in relation to what surrounds him (see
chapter 1). Sullivan enlarges this vision of the field to include the
evolutionary history of the person.

For Sullivan, the field was the arena in which interpersonal
relationships were being formed (Stern, 2015). Early on, he suggested that psychoanalysis should explore the interpersonal situation, in which the processes occur within the situation itself, which
is created between a subject and an observer, not within either the
subject or the observer (Sullivan, 1940). A person's individuality,
for him, remains inaccessible to science (Sullivan, 1940) because
personality is only observable in the interpersonal situation, which

DOI: 10.4324/9781003512844-9

includes the past and all the desires, fantasies and the most personal experiences of the patient.

The Hermeneutic Root of the Interpersonal Field

In the hermeneutic philosophy of Hans Georg Gadamer (1960), praxis is the primary guide, not the mere application of universal laws. The concern, typical in Gadamer, to not say too much, to never arrive at constructs that do not issue directly from experience, to never be satisfied with what we come to understand, to formulate, to interpret, but always to leave some door open, proves to be particularly important in our profession, in which it is necessary to dismiss the illusion of a knowledge possibly saturated with the reality in which we are immersed. The hermeneutic aspect of interpreting is not about the act of cognitive representation as much as the experience of "subjective perception" – that is, the thinking experience of human beings insofar as they are present in flesh and blood in the world.

From this perspective, there is the risk of falling into a kind of relativism – Hegel's bad infinity (1807) – in which one could never reach a conclusion. On this subject, Gadamer highlighted that his hermeneutic philosophy was not an absolute position but a path of experience: there is no principle higher than remaining open to dialogue.

The concept of the real in Gadamer is the experience of the game, in which the distinction between subject and object proves to be inadequate, just as the distinction between a subject that invents the game and/or participates in it and a subject who is merely a spectator. Therefore, the game is a happening in which subject and object submit to the same rules, which constitute the seriousness of the game. Such a *happening* is the most authentic representation of being, not in the sense of a presumed objectivity but because it always in the end gives rise to the discovery of a new quality of being, the discovery of its own value of truth.

Within this framework, when an event comes into being, it is not possible to establish what is mine and what is yours, the analyst and patient both being unconsciously involved in the process. A "happening" is created, a "third".

We can bring this concept into the analytical consulting room, in which the third, or the field, is generated between analyst and patient. The analytic field obviously comprises and includes the body, or if we wish the embodied experience, but it is not only made up of this but also of the fantasies that are generated through it and through solicitations to its own unconscious patterns.

The type of knowing belonging specifically to hermeneutic experience in Gadamer, thanks to Heidegger, is traced back to the Greek concept of *phronesis* – that type of understanding that develops on the basis of the knowledge of the specific situation rather than universal laws.

In essence, hermeneutic philosophy is understood not as an absolute position but as a path of experience in which what is important is keeping oneself open to dialogue.

Within this framework, Gadamer rehabilitates prejudices by asserting that they are not only the repository of ignorance but also represent the starting point from which we move, the conditions themselves of our knowing. *Interpreting the real is therefore about being a mediator between the text and all that it implies.*

On this subject, I think it's interesting to underscore the importance of the conceptual foundation of the psychoanalytical clinical process, given the constant concern, in Gadamer, of not saying too much, and to never arrive at constructs that do not issue directly from experience, to never be satisfied with what we come to understand, formulate, or interpret but always to leave some door open, by dismissing the illusion of a knowledge saturated with the psychic reality in which we are immersed.

Praxis thus becomes the primary guide, the guide par excellence, since theorizations cannot be considered as universal laws to be applied to therapeutic situations. As Stern never tires of saying in his book (1997), the hermeneutic conception helps us to never be content with what we have understood, formulated, interpreted.

Among the other principal inspirations of Godamer's hermeneutic philosophy we find the concept of "fusion of horizons" (Dottori, 1991, p. 420), for which a complete identification with the spirit of past time, an objective and complete reconstruction and therefore an exhaustive understanding of it, proves impossible. Not even the "fusion of horizons" can bring us to a complete reappropriation of alterity: at best we arrive at a "knowing of oneself in being other".

Thus, we arrive at the "hermeneutic circle", in other words, the structure of pre-comprehension – the presuppositions or prejudices that form the conditions of our understanding – form a kind of anticipation of knowing. Therefore, such presuppositions or prejudices guide our knowing, which is guided by the intuition of the full or perfect knowledge of the past (Dottori, 1991). Interpretation is thus forced to revert back to its own prejudices, either to confirm or negate them. The strength of the hermeneutic circle lies in this reverting back to itself, and this takes place inside its fusion of horizons.

Ultimately hermeneutic practice lies in understanding, interpreting, elucidating and finally comparing the present with the past (Dottori, 1991).

The being of all that can be understood is language; this kind of being pertains to historical consciousness, since all understanding and interpretation happens through language. It is also the means – the intermediary of our entire social being – which allow us to communicate. Language is the game we all play (Gadamer, 1960).

In conclusion: in the hermeneutic field, the other never gives him/herself in his/her absolute alterity, and for that reason, even when we understand the other, this other can only reveal him/herself in what is ours. This statement excludes any possible objectivity in human knowing.

The Field in Interpersonal Psychoanalysis

One of the fundamental assumptions of interpersonal psychoanalysis deals with the fact that the analyst and patient are continuously, inevitably, consciously and unconsciously in reciprocal interaction with each other: in essence, this is the interpersonal field.

It has to do with the reciprocal influence between people, and it determines what each participant might feel in the presence of the other, in particular the affective aspects of the experience. On this basis, the field is the overall total of all the influences, conscious and unconscious, which each of the analytic participants exercise over the other; it is the result of the way in which they deal with each other.

As we have just seen, the concept of the interpersonal field digs its roots deep into the hermeneutic thought of Hans Georg Gadamer. We have seen how the impossibility of differentiating between subject and subject, in a continuously open and non-conclusive happening, is mirrored within it.

Differences between Interpersonal Field and Intersubjective Field

It is very important to understand well the conceptual foundations upon which theories stand. I will specifically highlight the differences between interpersonal psychoanalysis and intersubjective psychoanalysis, even if they both fall under the same umbrella of relational psychoanalysis.

My intention and my hope is to try to underscore how certain basic conceptualizations inevitably influence one's own way of working analytically, by bringing to light some differences, some more subtle, some less subtle, in how to fulfill one's profession.

The theory of intersubjectivity is also a field theory, in that it aims to understand how psychological phenomena are formed in the encounter of subjectivities in interaction, not as products of intrapsychic mechanisms (Stolorow and Atwood, 1992). It derives directly from Kohut's psychology of the Self, and its major exponents are Robert Stolorow, George Atwood, Donna Orange, for whom intersubjectivity presupposes an evolutionary achievement, and Jessica Benjamin, who is chiefly concerned with victim/oppressor relationships.

The conceptual foundation at the base of intersubjectivism, especially that of Benjamin, is not however the hermeneutic principle just described, but rather the philosophical parabola of the master/slave relationship of Hegel's *Phenomenology of Spirit* (1807). In it we find a Self (the master, the *doer*) a Self (the slave, the *done to*). In this conception, we find that the Self, in order to assert its own existence, needs the opportunity to act and influence the other. In essence, the desire to be recognized guides the need for reciprocity. From this perspective, the deconstruction of the relationships of authority and dependency (the subject who knows, the object who becomes known) has a crucial importance for the psychoanalytic relationship (Benjamin, 2017).

As it is possible to observe, the two positions, the interpersonal and the intersubjective, are not so far apart, and of course they aren't the objectives of therapy. However, I would like to emphasize that the conceptual starting premise is instead very different, the hermeneutic one being relative to an occurrence in which one cannot distinguish who is doing what to the other, the intersubjective one being based on the opposite premise, namely that there exists a doer and there exists a done to, even if such roles can be interchangeable.

As far as I'm concerned, this has an extremely important impact on the clinical process. The use of the analyst's subjectivity can, in fact, be changed, acquire different potential meanings, because the methodological starting position *is* different. We will more fully address these themes when we deal with the noticeable similarities and differences between relational psychoanalysis and interpersonal psychoanalysis.

The fact remains that the hermeneutic field in every case concerns the image of a path to patiently follow right to the end, across all the obstacles and all the adversities of the itinerary, making the most of opportunities from all the encounters, and from all the possibilities for knowledge and dialogue it offers.

Chapter 7

Countertransference

The Concept of Countertransference

We have now arrived at a central tenet of interpersonal psycho-analysis, which applies it in keeping with its deepest meaning.

Since 1910 (Freud, 1910), the definition of countertransference has concerned that which surfaces in the doctor through the patient's ingress into his unconscious emotions.

I should like to emphasize how the first use of this concept as a diagnostic tool is due in reality to Helene Deutsch (1942), who made reference precisely to the experiences and feelings that the analyst undergoes in making the "what if" personality diagnosis. The diagnostic tool for recognizing one of the forms of schizo-phrenia, even if not so defined at the time, was precisely counter-transference, namely the emotions and experiences of the therapist.

Subsequently, Paula Heimann (1950) intuited the emotions awakened in the analyst from the impact with the patient are often much closer to the essence of the problem than his/her words. The analyst's immediate emotional response would therefore be a rather quick and sensitive indicator of the patient's unconscious processes and the precondition for effective and concrete interpretations.

With Racker (1968) and his considerations of complementary and concordant countertransference, the relationship between analyst and patient is more and more recognized as the basic structure of the analytic process and transference and counter-transference as the pillars of therapy.

DOI: 10.4324/9781003512844-10

Countertransference therefore became increasingly legitimized as a valuable instrument of understanding and investigation and is considered as the most dynamic way in which the patient's voice reaches us. Its value lies in the fact that it can represent not only the analyst's reaction to the patient but the way in which the analyst directly experiences the working of parts of the patient's personality within him/herself.

> Here one already grasps with clarity the link which is being recognized between the meaning of the analyst's emotions and the emergence of the preverbal dimension in development and in analysis. The patient's words can miss expressing precisely what is more important and which due to its poorly differentiated nature lies beyond words. The analyst's emotions, his countertransference, thus constitute a preferred perceptive channel to re-establish an impossible and deceptive understanding through language.
> (Albarella and Donadio, 1998, p. 10, my translation)

We have seen (chapters 2, 3, 4) how in the interpersonal conception, right from its origins, participating is inevitable. The countertransferential experiences are therefore considered a valuable source and also a preferred channel for deepening and attempting to decodify the transferential dynamics.

The notion itself of the analytical situation progresses like this, in a revolutionized, gradual but inexorable way, becoming a dense narrative, variously interwoven, predominantly unconscious.

Countertransference and Participant Observation

The conception of the relationship in interpersonal psychoanalysis is based on the concepts of the interpersonal field (see chapter 6) and of participant observation. The analyst is an integral part of the observed situation; he/she is a participant observer.

Irwin Hirsch (1990, 1995, 1996, 1998, 2008) is the interpersonal author who more than anyone has accumulated the legacies of Clara Thompson and Benjamin Wolstein in relation to these concepts. I have had the opportunity to sit in on his classes and conferences both at the White Institute and at several Forums of the APSA and in Florence, where we invited him to hold a seminar. An amiable and warm-hearted person, a writer of numerous articles and books, he has worked hard for the development of interpersonal psychoanalysis.

Hirsch (1996) observes that Sullivan had introduced the model of the *participant observer* based on Heisenberg's "uncertainty principle" (1927) and on the theories of social psychology, for which the observer, by definition, interacts and influences what he/she sees (see chapter 1), but he always avoided an explanation and the clinical use of his own countertransferential participation. This approach to the study emphasized the examination of the forces of interaction within a field, seen as agents constantly in action and subject to reciprocal influences.

The basis for a revision of the concept of countertransference and of the inevitability of the interaction in psychoanalysis had thus been established. Before Sullivan, in fact, countertransference had been seen as an impediment to the analytical process, as something to control if not eradicate.

A central premise of Interpersonal psychoanalysis inquiry is that each participant in psychoanalysis is involved as part of an interpersonal field in processes that invariably affect, and are affected by, that field of experience.

(Fiscalini, 1995b, p. 611)

At this point, one no longer just focusses on the patient and his/her suffering but especially on what occurs *between* patient and analyst. In essence, the analyst becomes part of what he/she intends to heal and is not someone who endorses what may be the correct meaning of what is happening. He/she ceases to be a neutral referee of the patient's transference. In fact, transference is not only the distortion or repetition of the past but also the *response to the real situation with the analyst*. Thus, the therapist's participation is recognized.

As we have seen in chapter 4, credit must be given to Clara Thompson for having emphasized the inevitable importance of countertransference, and for having maintained that it could be controlled by means of the analyst's attention and acceptance of his/her own subjectivity.

Starting with this theorization, countertransference would be considered useful, when not indispensable, for understanding the patient as an individual and as part of the transference/counter-transference matrix.

It must be emphasized that countertransference is no longer seen as a contamination of the therapeutic field but more precisely as one of the poles of the relationship, the facts of which become integrated with the patient's experience in defining the framework in constant development, in which the subjects are reciprocally immersed. What one is trying to attain is a further expansion of the facts which may clarify the continuity between past and present which the therapeutic situation produces. New connections of meaning are thus fostered, as we will see in Levenson's thinking (chapter 10).

It is surely due to the encounter of the two personalities in the analytical situation that specific and unique ways of being in therapy arise and demonstrate the centrality of the analyst's personality.

In conclusion, contemporary interpersonal psychoanalysts see countertransference as one of the analyst's greatest allies in the ana-lytic process. In fact, Feiner (1977) stated that if we do not see our countertransference, then we are basically abandoning the patient.

> This has led to a shift not only in the analyst's optimal use of self but in the view of the mutative action of therapy as well. Focus has changed from therapeutic action primarily as a function of objective and veridical interpretation to that of new affective experience between analysts and patient as the key to the patient's growth and enrichment. Interpersonal development in the theory and clinical use of counter-transference has led to a more vulnerable analyst, in that the patient can no longer be viewed as the source of all of the interaction in the transference-countertransference exchange. With this increased vulnerability, however, come much addi-tional data for the analyst to bring into the primary task of expanding and enriching the life of the patient.
>
> (Hirsch, 1995, p. 657)

Section III

Chapter 8

Clinical Theory

Trauma in Interpersonal Psychoanalysis: A Synthesis

Interpersonal psychoanalysis, with its roots in the theories of Harry Stack Sullivan, places emphasis on interpersonal relationships as the foundation of personality and psychopathology. Within this context, trauma is not exclusively seen as a single isolated event, but rather as a pattern of negative and repeated relational experiences which can leave deep psychological wounds.

Trauma, therefore, is mediated by interpersonal relationships, and the emotional and behavioral responses to a traumatic event are influenced by the way in which the individual relates to significant others throughout life. Thus, it can establish dysfunctional relational patterns that are repeated over time, which can lead to difficulties in emotional regulation, in the building of intimate relationships, and in the trusting of others, interfering in this way with the development of a cohesive and positive self-image.

The individual can internalize the negative aspects of traumatic relationships, developing an inadequate sense of self and one full of shame. In particular, traumatic experiences in the early stages of life, especially those tied to the figure of attachment, can have a particularly deep impact on personality development and on vulnerability to trauma (see chapter 3) because the experience of absolute privation and the dimensions of emptiness prevent the integration of one's own mental processes with interactive processes. It is from this type of trauma, which produces intolerable angst, that the not-me experiences arise; this represents the

DOI: 10.4324/9781003512844-12

interpersonal genesis of dissociation. The experience in these cases remain non-formulated and therefore dissociated.

Trauma can contribute to the development or the exacerbation of numerous mental disorders, such as post-traumatic stress disorder (PTSD), borderline personality disorder, depression, generalized anxiety, panic attacks and specific phobias.

The treatment of trauma in interpersonal psychoanalysis presents extremely interesting elements. Naturally, the creation of a safe environment is fundamental in the treatment of patients who have suffered traumas, so that they feel welcome and can express their emotions in a safe way. The main objectives consist of helping the patient to understand how past traumatic experiences influence his/her way of thinking, feeling and behaving in the present, through a deep understanding of the connections that emerge, in order to identify and then modify the dysfunctional relational patterns that have emerged following the trauma. This process strengthens the patient's internal resources, like self-esteem, resilience and the ability to deal with stress.

What is specifically interpersonal is the conception of the past that permeates the treatment style and includes the theory of the unconscious to which we refer. Obviously, through the narration and the re-evocation of memories, the patient can work through the traumatic experiences and attribute a new meaning to them. But for the interpersonal analyst, the past does not have importance in itself. It does not possess an intrinsic reality: it is not about reliving the traumatic event through a regression facilitated by the therapist, a kind of Alexander-style "corrective emotional experience" (Alexander and French, 1946), and this is so for more than one reason. Above all, the past is not dredged up out of the sea of the unconscious just as it was in the patient's reality. We are no longer dealing with an operation of the archaeological kind, in which I retrieve an experience, buried in the unconscious, and I relive it exactly as it was, perhaps shrugging off the dust and the rust deposited there. Since we are speaking of dissociated experiences (see chapter 5), they are not accessible through regression, which implies a static conception of the unconscious, where the repressed item manifests itself once again, like a hidden object which taken away from its hiding-place remains the same object, only now it is visible. Instead, they are revealed, if we are lucky, only in the relationship with the analyst, through enactments.

We will learn more about these concepts in the next chapter.

Enactment

The enactment represents a central concept of interpersonal psychoanalysis, acquiring a relevant meaning in the exploration of the relational dynamics between patient and therapist. It proves to be extremely useful in terms of therapeutic objectives because it represents *the interpersonalization of dissociation.*

We have an unconscious reciprocal enactment when analyst and patient have dissociative patterns that become tightly intertwined with each other. There exist clear examples of these interactions, which take place when anger, shame or envy spring up between two individuals who do not perceive them, who are not in contact with what they are feeling, being unconscious and dissociated; they live it as the "not-me", and this is why at best they could swear that it is the other one having that feeling (Stern, 1997). Such experiences, therefore, in view of the fact that patients have no means by which they can reference them, can only find their own way through enactments. In psychotherapy and in psychoanalysis, these enactments, or "dead ends", are simultaneously the most dangerous parts and potentially the most useful in treatment.

Resolution of the enactments is a fundamental aspect of psychoanalytic treatment. In turn, it requires a rupture in the dissociations which lie at their base, a rupture that is manifested generally through a new perception of the other.

The analyst also dissociates, just as the patient does. The rupture of the dissociations which is necessary so that the enactment may get resolved is usually initiated by the analyst, but the opposite can also occur – that is, the work can be done together to unravel the tangle in which they have become bound. The significant difference between the two participants is not to be found in the relative seriousness of their respective psychopathologies but *in the type of position that they assume towards their own experience*: analysts for this reason must face extensive training and are trained in having the ability to listen (Stern, 2013, 2015).

From the interpersonal point of view, the enactment is defined as an *absence* of sufficient conflict, in the opposite direction to which much of contemporary psychoanalysis leads; the resolution of an enactment will require the *creation* of a conscious conflict where there was no trace of one before (being in the not-me). According to this perspective, the conscious conflict is the *only* form of conflict, inasmuch as the unconscious conflict is not accessible, given that the unconscious experience is not formulated, and therefore has not assumed that kind of explicit form which would render it possible to be in conflict with any other aspect of the experience (see chapter 9).

In short, the enactment in interpersonal psychoanalysis is configured as a relational phenomenon which, if adequately recognized and used, becomes a potent vehicle of insight and therapeutic change. It requires constant vigilance and self-reflection on the part of the therapist, so as to allow an effective management of the relational dynamics which emerge in the therapeutic context.

Self-revelation, Self-disclosure and/or Disclosure of the Analytic Process

We have already shed light many times on the hypothesis according to which clinical work improves when one abandons the analyst's aspiration to neutrality. We no longer ask ourselves "if" countertransference may provide information on the patient and on the interaction with him/her, but rather "if, when and how much" of what countertransference evokes might be introduced in the direct exchange with the patient.

In particular, interpersonal psychoanalysis supports the need for the analyst to meticulously monitor his/her own reactions, including memories and spontaneous associations, revealed to the patient when the analyst maintains their usefulness to the objectives of the treatment (Levenson, 1996).

In the meantime, let us clarify the meaning of the following terms:

1) For self-revelation we mean a passive act. To reveal signifies making known what was previously hidden. Self-revelation is inevitable and concerns all the information on him/herself

that the therapist cannot give, and which is inherent in his/her own physicality, style, décor of the consulting room, linguistic inflections, social background and interests, etc.

2) For self-disclosure we mean a real action. To disclose signifies acting. Making known an event which has been taken into consideration but, for valid reasons, has not been fully revealed.

Self-disclosure therefore concerns everything the therapist deliberately decides to show or say to the patient.

1) Self-revelation is therefore inevitable, and within it there is no initiative on the part of the therapist.

The first important issue that arises is: to what extent is it worth validating the patient's discoveries, in other words, in using self-disclosure (an action) as a means of controlling self-revelation (an experience)? Citing Gill (1983), a writer among the most famous to have converted to the impersonal model, and Levenson (1996), one of its most eminent representatives, both unequivocally advise confirming the perception of the patient.

Personally, I fully agree with them because in this way one confirms to the patient that his perception of the world is worth being considered, thus contributing to the expansion of his self-awareness, which, in fact, always develops consensually. Respecting the patient's perception means accepting that he/she is perhaps seeing what you yourself do not consciously see and feel. In fact, these possible feelings and experiences could also unconsciously be appropriate responses to something that really concerns the patient, responses that can be effectively and subsequently used, if one knows how to wait for clarifying experiences to occur.

2) We have said that when it comes to self-disclosure, a deliberate action by the analyst is understood, a revealing of something about him/herself to the patient.

Here one can become perplexed in that many writers generate confusion in the reader because they often indiscriminately use the words self-disclosure and disclosure, as if they had the same meaning. There wouldn't be anything bad if everyone conventionally intended this, but placing the "self" before the noun cannot but indicate something more precise, which pertains to the analyst's subjectivity (Loiacono, 2016).

Many authors, in fact, prefer, for example, to speak about the disclosure of the analyst's subjectivity (Cooper, 1998), or about countertransferential disclosure (Bollas, 1983; Ehrenberg, 1995; Greenberg, 1986), distinguishing it from self-disclosure. We will return to this subject shortly.

In the meantime, we will adopt the use of the single word disclosure here. In other words, I will refer to the deliberate choice of the analyst to reveal something about himself to the patient without using the word self-disclosure, except in the case in which I will cite colleagues who use it. This is the reason for my choice: either we maintain that the analyst, in his/her relationship with the patient, can keep a portion of his/her Self outside of the relationship itself (and therefore it would be appropriate to speak of self-disclosure – that is, he/she chooses to reveal something of his/her own self absolutely disconnected from the analytical relationship, not inherent or related to it) or we maintain that any type of revelation we choose to make to the patient, being as we are entirely involved within the relational matrix of the patient him/herself – something that contributes to our therapeutic impact – cannot help but concern the self of the analyst in this matrix, and therefore also concern the relationship itself.

It seems to me that otherwise it would reify something – namely the Self – which one cannot objectify without paying a price for it later on, both on the theoretical level and on the technical level. In fact, it would then seem that one was allowing what one had thrown out of the door to come back in through the window – that is, the possibility of the neutrality of the analyst in the relationship – in some way the ability to describe and circumscribe a part of his/her Self, which, even though within the relationship with the patient remains outside of it. All in all, a contradiction in terms.

Disclosure, therefore, concerns a specific response in a specific context, generated within the narrowest frame of the intersubjective field.

Self-revelation, self-disclosure and disclosure are thus to be considered as dimensions of the analyst/patient relationship. Now we must raise the most important issue of them all – the use value that they can have in therapy (Loiacono, 2016).

A Clinical Example

I am including here a vignette to help facilitate the understanding of the problematic nature of the issue and to arouse interest in this discussion.

The vignette I have chosen concerns a session with a thirty-four-year-old depressed patient in analysis with me for two years because he had attempted suicide twice. During the session in question, in which I was privately noticing how in the last while interacting with him had become more vital and how his tone of voice was much less "listless" than usual (I felt that a more vigorous process had been set in motion), I was aware of having used the familiar form of the second person singular while I was speaking – the "*tu*" in Italian; I did not highlight the fact, and neither did he, although I felt that he took note of it, and it seemed to me that it pleased him.

In subsequent sessions, I was careful to pick up if in some way this had possibly triggered something. As a matter of fact, the following sessions marked an important process of change in which the patient stopped being the oedipal son and began to feel able to contend with aggressivity: from castrated in terms of independence, he was starting to grow again. I am sure that a large part of the unconscious processing that this patient was doing from that episode in a matter of weeks was a response to that "*tu*" that had escaped me.

If I had instead chosen to verbalize the occurrence, motivating him with my unconscious response to the fact I was beginning to sense him as a man and no longer as a frightened child abandoned by his mother (his birth mother was psychotic; she had committed suicide when he was six, and he had been entrusted to another family), of course I would have been sincere and transparent, and perhaps, but we will never know, I would have set other dynamics in motion. I chose, instead, not to do it, although I gradually realized, but after the fact, that at the very least a large part of the patient's processing had emanated from that "*tu*". If I had opted for self-disclosure, if I had emphasized it and had also made explicit my underlying experience, I believe I would have made the situation more conflictual by inserting within it my person in an intrusive and narcissistic way. If the process had been blocked and I had seen our patient close himself off and become scared, the outcome would have been different; in that case I would have absolutely intervened, in the first place asking him to what extent his sudden withdrawal could have been connected to my "*tu*", and, if necessary, in service of the process, certainly revealing the change in my perception of him in the last sessions, moving on to analyze the manner of his emotional responses to such a change. When, however, the flow moves forward without any blockage, I find myself more in agreement with those who prefer not to interrupt it, so as not to unnecessarily neuroticize the field.

The subjectivity of the analyst in his/her interaction with the patient and his/her implicit influence within the relationship with the patient absolutely persist whether we choose to verbalize them or not.

But, as I am writing, I realize that, as always, the analyst's personal style, the respect he/she has for the patient and him/herself, the analyst's technical and theoretical competence and capacity for empathy (directly dependent on the working through of his/her own narcissism), are the fundamental coordinates of a relational analyst, and an interpersonal one in particular, not the way in which we choose to "reveal ourselves" (Loiacono, 2016).

Before moving towards the conclusion, I will briefly refer to other writers.

Some propose the use of self-disclosure as the key tool of "laying one's cards on the table" with the patient, propelling the rejection of the old concept of neutrality to extreme consequences. Renik (1999), for example, maintains that the more the analyst recognizes and is available to discuss his/her own personal presence in the therapeutic situation, the less space he/she occupies, and therefore more space is left for the patient. The analyst desirous of neutrality easily ends up personifying the unreachable Sphinx, proposing a pathological interactive space of a narcissistic type.

Others favor instead the use of the single word "disclosure". Among them, we should recall those who speak of "transferential disclosure", such as Bollas (1983), who believes that disclosure is central for increasing the patient's ability to experience transference through the therapist's revelations in the moments that he/she chooses, around his/her own subjective experience of the interaction; Ehrenberg (1995), who considers it a way to attain understanding rather than the result of a rigorous examination. If he senses instead a clear understanding of his countertransferential reactions, he abstains from disclosure, or, at any rate, he does not feel obliged to disclose; and J. Greenberg (1986), who considers disclosure an important technical tool for facilitating the strengthening of the necessary neutrality, which he views as the position capable of promoting an optimal tension between being seen as a new and an old object (*something old, something new*).

I will take advantage of this opportunity to cite Levenson once again. He advises the use of self-disclosure for that which concerns the dreams that the analyst has about the patient but specifies that it is however necessary to be careful and to use it only in cases of a stabilized therapeutic alliance (see chapter 10).

It appears evident that it is impossible to reach a consensus on the presented issues. My intention has been to explain the importance of reflecting on the different positions.

Angst as a "Presence of Feeling"

A well-known Italian psychoanalyst, Leonardo Ancona, wrote that

> angst is applicable to a substantially different psychic process than that of anxiety. In fact, angst corresponds to a trauma situation, that is to an influx of uncontrollable excitations, because they are too large within the unit of time [...]. Anxiety corresponds on the other hand to a process of adaptation in the face of a threat of a realistic danger; this process is a function of the Ego, which uses it as a signal, after having

produced it, to avoid being submerged by the traumatic influx of excitations. In this case, the Ego of the subject is active, in that it produces affect and uses it to find adequate mechanisms for defense; the drive capacity becomes structuralized and reproduced without an economic base, in other words without the implementation of a discharge. The distinction between the two processes is maintained, interpreting their unification as an aspect of a culture that presents, in the face of this subject matter, less sensitivity for a probable defensive attitude on this matter. The processes to which we are referring are in reality distinct from the economic, dynamic, structural point of view as well as the genetic one. Therefore, disregarding this distinction produces contradictoriness and confusion.

(Ancona, 1972, p. 918, my translation)

In line with Ancona's considerations, which are still fundamental today in the examination of the combined usage or not of the two terms, I have chosen in this work to use the term "angst" rather than "anxiety" because angst of the integrative type to which I refer pertains to a traumatic situation. In fact, we are dealing with angst which accompanies the process of integration of not-me personifications (Loiacono, 2019).

Angst without Affect

Gregory Zilboorg (1933) tried to understand the way in which angst is manifested without affect in many neurotic patients and in many so-called normal people. He observed that affect sometimes appears to be so elusive that in order to avoid it coming into the open the patient can feign its *real motor expression* in the hope that, as it moreover often occurs, it is mistaken for genuine feeling (what comes to mind here is the "as if" personality of Deutsch (1942)). The evasion of angst-inducing affect is a specific modality of the splitting of the affect, whose goal is that of avoiding psychic pain. (In this case, Zilboorg speaks correctly of splitting and not dissociation, navigating a different theoretical context than the interpersonal one.)

In keeping with Zilboorg, an angst-ridden reaction is formed by three components: ideational content, affective tone (affect) and motor reaction. The ideational content can also appear by itself, when the affective tone and the motor expression are repressed, as one can observe in certain forms of obsessiveness. It can also happen that the affective tone is at the forefront while the ideational content remains repressed, but on these occasions the motor accompaniment would then also be present, as for example any type of neurotic anxiety crisis; during such a crisis, the subject is aware of his/her own angst (affect) and shows this through his/her pallor, trembling, acceleration of the heartbeat and respiratory frequency etc. – in other words, through the motor component.

From this angle, fear would therefore be the signal of an "absent feeling"; it would express an "angst without affect", namely, dissociated angst that is manifested through raw sensations of fear towards something. The eruption of angst as affect that is perceived without the need for an ascribed object, therefore, becomes integrative angst, from this standpoint, which I propose to call a "present feeling", in opposition to the other, Zilboorg's absent feeling, which pertains to the domination of fear. In essence: fear allows for the avoidance of pain. Entering into contact with pain presupposes a perception of angst, signaling the integration of the dissociated material (Loiacono, 2019).

The goal of the following clinical material is to show how the appearance of the perception of the angst-ridden feeling may be considered a turning point in the therapeutic process, the beginning of a sense of vitality, a kind of re-awakening.

Clinical Examples

Myriam comes with a dream:

> I am in analysis here in the consulting room with you, but you are about to go with your partner – or husband, I'm not sure – to have an aperitif. For this reason, you have gathered together all the patients so as to be free early. I was feeling indescribable angst. I was feeling really bad. You realize that I'm feeling bad. You approach me and say: 'next week I won't

be here, but I promise that we will recoup that session'. [It is worthwhile noting that generally speaking I never speak about recouping a session. A missed session for me is lost. Besides which, it would be like her to miss the following session for an umpteenth trip that she was about to take. Myriam is often absent.] 'I feel calm and reassured immediately, the stabbing pain is no longer there because you realized that I was feeling badly'.

This dream, which occurred after a year and a half of therapy, highlights, besides the entrance of oedipal themes, a theme which characterized analysis with Myriam: the need to avoid angst. Myriam can experience fear but resorts to all possible expedients in order not to "feel" the angst she is experiencing.

I will now recount another example taken from my clinical practice, to draw attention to the vast range of situations that typically occur with patients who use dissociative modalities.

Irene, a thirty-five-year-old patient, has been in analysis with me for dissociative episodes, the last one of which persisted over an entire week of continuous feelings of depersonalization, and through which it seemed to her as if she was living as if detached, in a different place from the one she was in. This caused her to make the decision to begin therapy.

After around two years, she came to me with this dream:

I am here with you in a session, but many emotionally significant others come in with me – my family, my friends, and they are here conversing. The first time I don't say anything even if I had things to say to you and I'm a little upset. The second time I am aware of allowing myself to sink down more and more in the armchair, until I am almost completely lying down, while the others are talking. Then, all of a sudden, I get a grip on myself and, extremely angry with you, I tell you to send them away, I say that we will make up these two sessions without counting them because I want them back.

The associations concern the previous session, during which she spoke to a great extent about her sister and about how she greedily takes everything for herself.

Irene tells me that she has the feeling that she wasted all the time of the session, and she wonders why I let her do that. So, I put the facts before her that she had obviously brought to the session an unconscious pattern which takes up a large part of her internal world.

After my words, it was as if she had been shaken, and, bursting into tears, she said that in fact she went back to feeling the pain and sense of loneliness precisely after the previous session. First, she felt detached from what was happening to her. At most, in the evening before going to sleep, she felt some emotion, perhaps shed a tear, but then she was asleep and felt again detached in the morning. Now she needs to cry. She is experiencing pain.

Patients like Myriam and Irene, in my opinion, represent the contemporary clinical situation, where we encounter people who bring us their detachment, sometimes even total, from their emotions, from their fears. They seem incapable of being in contact with their own existential dimension, stubbornly committed as they are to avoiding feeling pain, to avoiding suffering.

We are essentially witnessing dissociation from the feeling of angst, which therefore appears and is revealed to the clinician's eyes in the form of detachment, or else through mere acting, and in any case the feeling that it generates whether it be detachment or its opposite, as for example a hypomanic reaction, has the result of being "absent" and is not perceived. Angst can thus be avoided; it seems "absent", but a whole range of raw emotions is experienced, ones which are connected to it, like fear, terror, panic, detachment, apathy, etc.

Once the dissociated material has been integrated, the work consists of then fostering a processing through which the patient can eventually transform the integrated personifications, no longer dissociated. Generally speaking, this happens gradually through enactments, a working through them and overcoming them (Hirsch, 1998, 2008; Stern, 1997, 2010; Buechler, 2017). All this work enables the perception of the wound (or wounds) as something situated in the past and no longer in the present. Thus, it finally becomes possible to restore the good parts of the primary object and recognize one's own identification with the primary object itself (Loiacono, 2019).

The Analyst's Subjectivity from the Contemporary Interpersonal Perspective

The issue of the subject and subjectivity has been debated for a long time, first in philosophy and then in psychoanalysis, and is multifaceted. In this context, I will refer to it in the sense of the analyst's therapeutic identity, which is based on the "personal equation" of which Racker has spoken (1968), namely a *personal identity* which proves to be a specific tool with exceptional use value because it is capable of achieving quick decisional processes in a probabilistic system with a high degree of uncertainty (Loiacono, 2010, 2021).

Let us recall the words of Freud himself when he tells us that one can learn how to make opening moves in chess, but the way in which the game proceeds is linked to experience, to the characteristics of that particular person who is playing that game (Freud, 1913).

As we have said more than once within the consulting room (and quite often even outside of it), the analyst and the patient are always, inevitably, part of the experience of the other, consciously and unconsciously. Analytic work (diagnosis, understanding the patient's history, deciding about the end of analysis) therefore inevitably reflects the subjectivity of the analyst, which reveals itself to be a fundamental tool for activating and making the analytic process valuable and fruitful.

Chapter 9

The Unformulated Experience

The first time I met Donnel B. Stern was in October 2003. I was especially struck by the clinical implications of his statements on the *unformulated experience* (1983). What particularly reverberated within me was his ability to put into words (by examining them) the difficulties that one most often encounters in the relationship with patients: what to do with what Stern calls "spontaneous perceptions" in analysis, and which for the most part make up our daily work? How do we manage to go beyond the chains and limitations imposed by transference and countertransference? How can the eye see itself? How can the self-reflective experience, what Stern defines as the "enigmatic act", become formulated?

In the summer of 2005, I went to New York to do a cycle of supervisions with him. From this experience was born the idea of translating into Italian his book on unformulated experience. As president of the then Italian Society for Interpersonal Psychoanalysis (SIPI), I organized a conference with him on this subject in Florence in October 2007, to coincide with the publication of his book in Italian.

It was not easy for me to understand this theory, because I had in mind those theories of the unconscious that I was used to always considering, and without realizing it, I wished to find a collocation for this concept within my preexisting assumptions. Imagining that this could happen as well to someone who is reading this book, I will therefore begin by giving a general picture of the theories of the unconscious which we are used to adopting, in the hope of thus bringing the reader immediately into

DOI: 10.4324/9781003512844-13

contact with this theory, which represents a *radical alternative* to the dynamic unconscious of Freud.

Evolution of the Theories of the Unconscious

The physiognomy of the unconscious has changed over time, becoming increasingly an adjective, rather than a noun, and increasingly relational.

We can say that for Freud it had the function of unleashing drives, while for contemporary psychoanalysis it has the function of forming and preserving bonds with others.

For Freud, psychic contents (ideas, desires, unconscious beliefs, etc.) remain the same when they are either unconscious or when they become conscious. Like a hidden object that removed from its hiding place remains the same object (see chapter 8).

In essence, for contemporary psychoanalysis, for which ideas and desires have lost importance given that it has rejected the drive theory, the idea itself of an unconscious as a reservoir of already formed contents is unsustainable. The interest is completely focused on implicit processes (Eagle, 2011).

Contemporary psychoanalysis, relational and interpersonal, is in fact oriented towards mainly considering the pathologizing and traumatic relationships. As a result, the boundary between conscious and unconscious appears much more fluid with respect to Freud's barrier of repression because it is directly related to an analytical relationship which allows for exploration and giving shareable and verbalizable meaning to the unconscious configurations. Instead of an onion to peel, we have a kaleidoscope in which continuously changeable configurations are formed (Davies, 1996).

In the relational unconscious, three categories of experience can be identified:

1   desires and fantasies relative to the object, which become unacceptable in the context of a real or phantasmatic dual relationship (it is the aspect closest to the classical unconscious);
2   experiences of the Self which are incompatible and irreconcilable with aspects of the other and which due to their irreconcilability cannot be simultaneously conscious;

3 aspects of the experience of the self, which by their very nature are excluded from the linguistic categorization of a generalizable experience.

Stolorow and Atwood (1992) propose in turn three interconnected forms of the unconscious:

1 the pre-reflective unconscious, that is: the organizing principles that model and thematize the individual's experiences;
2 the dynamic unconscious, that is: the experiences to which expression has been denied because they put indispensable bonds in danger;
3 the unvalidated unconscious, that is: the experiences that could not be expressed because they never elicited the necessary validating response on the part of the environment.

The constantly dynamic aspect, in the making, of the relational conscious, not only allows one to be able to "have new eyes", of Proustian memory, but also as much as, and I believe above all, to be able to create a space in which painful experiences that are uncommunicable, unthinkable and stored in implicit memory can be representable. Against this background, the journey in itself acquires enormous importance, which, therefore, is characterized as always open to the search for gradually less and less rigid meanings, and which can become transformable and shareable.

But what are the ways in which the unconscious of the patient and that of the analyst manifest themselves and come into contact? The method for exploring the unconscious is still based on the patient's free associations and on the analyst's free-floating attention, and on giving meaning to somatic manifestations, a lapsus, a parapraxis (Freudian slip), a dream. Today however we also make use of new concepts like reverie, in which the analyst directs his/her floating attention to his/her own freely emerging thoughts, and also, as in the technique employed in child psycho-analysis, modeled on play, on drawing, on action in the session. Besides these, the latest neuropsychological discoveries give us reason to talk about two systems of memory: the explicit, subject to memory and verbalizable, and the implicit, not subject to memory and non-verbalizable. These observations have allowed for a revision and expansion of the concept of the unconscious, downsizing that aspect of it linked to repression, in favor of non-repressed experiences.

It is this that allows us today to see *the unconscious as a function of the mind characterized by fantasies and defenses*, among which stand out splitting and projective identification, and dissociation with respect to early relational traumas, deposited in implicit memory and therefore pre-symbolic and non-verbalizable.

The paths to access the unconscious have not changed – dreams, lapses, (Freudian) slips, transference, non-verbal modalities, etc. – as much as the way to read and interpret them. It is here that the concept of the unconscious that each current of thought and, in the final analysis, each therapist carries within reveals itself to be central and can completely modify the therapeutic work.

It is noteworthy that throughout the entire relational sphere the analytical encounter does not consist only of the relationship between two people but also, perhaps especially, between their unconscious.

On this subject, interpersonal psychoanalysis maintains that the analyst's participation is *involuntary*, namely that even the analyst cannot avoid acting according to the patterns relative to his/her unconscious. The analyst will be able only afterwards, through his/her self-reflective orientation, to understand and interpret how much and which influence his/her experiences have drawn from his/her own unconscious and that of the patient.

The intersubjective current of thought, which considers central the empathic mental attitude and the function of the object-Self of the analyst, maintains that such dispositions are instead consciously assumed.

The Unformulated Experience

D. B. Stern's *unformulated experience* represents instead a radical alternative to Freud's dynamic unconscious and is the only theory of the unconscious directly resulting from the interpersonal conception of the mind's dissociative functioning.

In fact, for Stern, if a psychic content is unconscious, it means that it is not articulated. It does not have a defined form. They are still unthought thoughts or not yet established connections. These contents can become unconscious by formulating the not-yet-formulated, that which is still in raw form – non-verbal, not articulated – giving it form through words. In essence, giving status to the non-verbal by means of the verbal.

The concept of repression and the concept of the unconscious are challenged. In this area, Stern is profoundly influenced by the philosophy of Herbert Fingarette (1963, 1969), according to whom individuals do not make explicit some elements of their personal contribution to things in order to avoid angst, a sense of guilt or other aspects of the self which they do not wish to acknowledge – a conception he calls "of the hidden reality" of unconscious psychic contents (self-deception).

Clinical Example

A patient of mine relates to me that one of the men with whom she often has occasional sex made her stay the night and sleep with him, but then in the morning he didn't even bring her a cup of coffee in bed, even though he came back into the bedroom with one for himself. He was just waiting for her to leave. During the sexual encounter, and in the night, he was rather sweet with her although not loving, but she felt hurt by his behavior over the unoffered coffee or invitation to eat together the evening before. I ask her if she ever pointed this out to him, and she looked at me stunned: she had never thought of it! Even with her current boyfriend, or rather someone she has been seeing for a certain period of time, the same thing is happening. She never knows if she will see him the following evening, and she doesn't ask if he misses her when he is away. She doesn't say this to him, nor does she tell him that she wishes to see him when he is around. When I question her as to why she doesn't settle the issue as suggested by me, and why she acts as if it were natural to behave by silencing her own desires and emotions, she answers that she has never thought of it in these terms. When I mention to her that her way of presenting herself could also communicate distance and/or disinterest on her part, she is speechless. Then she understands and tells me that she can't think of any reason why a man might love her. It is obvious that they would behave this way. She doesn't refuse an overture even when she is not interested because she cannot deny herself. Later on in analysis, it comes out that her mother always told her that she wasn't wanted, and she can't believe how she could have grown up given that, up until she was five to six years old, unfortunately both her mother and her husband were totally engaged in trying to make the imminent death of their only son, afflicted with a serious illness, as painless as possible.

The Unconscious Influence

These are the questions which D. B. Stern poses:

> When we refer to unconscious influence in psychoanalysis, what do we mean? Do we intend to refer to an objective presence in psychic life, a thought or an affect or a memory that somehow exists as a fact, but outside our ken? Or do we intend to refer to an absence, something missing in experience, an unconsidered or undeveloped implication?
>
> (Stern, 1997, p. 33)

Is the unconscious material really only waiting to be revealed, or is it the potential experience which must yet be expressed and justified?

Did the interpretation that is restored to the patient exist before the analyst's intervention? Did it exist before the patient was capable of putting it into words?

We are used to looking at dreams, lapses, symptoms, transference, parapraxes (Freudian slips) as evidence of the unconscious, of the non-verbal. Through interpretation we presume that we have clarified unconscious meanings. And yet, we often feel unsatisfied. We aren't sure of having captured this or that content. There remains a sort of deviation between what we have managed to put into words and some sensations that we barely perceive.

It is here that the concept of the unformulated experience takes shape: there are no thoughts that are simply waiting to be discovered and formulated. On the contrary, we find ourselves in that state of uncertainty about how to proceed, as if we have been enveloped by fog and we have allowed ourselves to be guided only by small signals that we seem to glimpse.

> The moments of confusion may be quite brief, barely notice-able, or they may be lengthy, becoming either deeply intriguing or disturbing. 'Unformulated experience' is the label I have chosen to refer to mentation characterized by lack of clarity and differentiation. Unformulated experience is the uninterpreted form of those raw materials of conscious, reflective experience that may eventually be assigned verbal interpretation and thereby brought into articulate form.
>
> (Stern, 1997, p. 37)

The resolution of the ambiguity of the unformulated experience is always an interpersonal event. Whether the process of symbolization takes place or not depends on the interpersonal context in which the problem could emerge.

Stern tells us that the unconscious should be conceived as something more than a mere container, and it does not have a structurally predefined content but lives and is made explicit in the psychic happening of the relationship, by achieving a structuring of its own meanings through the verbal experience in dialogue between people. He considers the unconscious a valuable resource which offers material for reflection, material with which to carry out its own evolutive task (Stern, 1997).

The interpersonal field (chapter 6) defines which part of our pre-reflective experience can be put into words and therefore thought, and which, on the other hand, will always remain closed outside of it. Understanding and interpretation are developed through a reciprocal interpersonal influence and the relational experience configures the possible experiential meanings. The patient's life story is also in part a new story that is being created within the interaction with the analyst, of the past "fusion of horizons" of the analyst and analysand.

The hermeneutic concept of fusion of horizons applied to the analytical relationship is for Stern that which is expressed in the clinical interpretation or in the attainment of empathy, a possibility in which the patient acquires the ability to understand him/herself and the experience of the analyst.

To access the "hermeneutic circle", in other words understanding of the context, the analyst must remain open to treating the context or prejudice as a hypothesis, always keeping a certain indispensable degree of uncertainty. Basically, this is totally aligned with Gadamer's thinking on the process of understanding.

The opposite of the hermeneutic circle is the vicious circle: the analyst is not aware of being mostly engaged in finding proof for what he/she already believes he/she knows, thus imposing his/her perspective on the patient. In this case, there is no reciprocity but only a *monologue masquerading as dialogue* (Stern, 2002). The distinctiveness of Stern's thinking on this lies in the fact that he traces the origins of this possibility (the vicious circle) to the outcome of a dissociation between the states of the analyst's self.

Unformulated Experience and Weak and Strong Dissociation

Dissociation is the link that unifies the hermeneutic and the unformulated experience. The unformulated experience is to dissociation what the unconscious content is to repression. Here, therefore, dissociation is manifested in an enactment (see chapter 8) and consists of the impossibility of reflecting upon the experience and not of the unconscious avoidance of contact with the experience (Stern, 1997).

> when the interpersonal field is configured in a way that allows it, a fully formed meaning can emerge. Clinical psychoanalysis is devoted to the recognition and encouragement of such opportunities.
>
> (Stern, 2019, p. 7)

He explicitly identifies two possible qualities of dissociation: a "weak" dissociation, or *narrative rigidity*, namely the involvement in a narrative line so exclusive as to disregard or even prevent the expression of alternative possibilities; and a "strong" dissociation, namely a specifically defensive dissociation, employed to prevent an experience to be consciously felt. To break this *hold on the field* – in other words, the way in which dissociation has saturated the interpersonal field – we need the enactment to pertain to a weak dissociation.

> The stereotypic use of language is always dissociative, because it precludes new experience; the creative use of language just as surely and dependably results in the articulation of new experience, because creative language wants to accomplish nothing else. [...] the question is only whether the interpretation is hackneyed or from the heart.
>
> Dissociation in the strong sense refers to an active defensive process, an unconscious avoidance of the verbal articulation of certain kinds of experience that already have some kind of nonlinguistic unconscious structure – experience that exists as action or practice, such as transference and counter-transference. [...] At other times, the meaning in question is not specifically disavowed at all, and is entirely implicit; it simply has never been attended in such a way that it could be formulated. Here the dissociative act occurs in the weak form.
>
> (Stern, 2019, pp. 113–114)

And later on:

> Dissociation is not necessarily limited to the absolute prevention of experience; it often merely drains experience of the feeling and the potential for narrative vigor that even the most terrible memory must have to be real.
>
> (Stern, 2019, p. 126)

On this matter, I advise reading Stern's illustration of several clinical cases (Stern, 2019, pp. 141–144, pp. 197–199).

When two people with similar dissociative patterns feel so crushed as to sense the threat of the undeniable presence within themselves of an intolerable experience, the result is an unconscious reciprocal enactment.

The resolution of the enactments thus assumes a fundamental place in psychoanalytical treatment (see chapter 8). During the enactment, each participant is literally dominated by one single way of perceiving him/herself and the other.

The resolution of an enactment coincides with a new perception of the other, a new non-verbal experience, which is then brought back into the verbal, through the sharing of meaning expressed through words. Verbal insight, however, remains secondary – what is crucial does not occur by means of words but adheres to the non-verbal.

Double and Triple Hermeneutic

Finally, there is another concept meriting attention. For Stern, the analyst has two hermeneutic tasks: one consists of being able to grasp at the implicit level the common daily meanings that the field has; the other, subsequent to this, concerns being able to understand how to be able to assimilate these meanings within one's own theoretical perspective, which constantly plays a crucial role in molding our perceptions and our prejudices. This is the concept of the *double hermeneutic* of A. Giddens (1976). Taking inspiration from this concept, Stern introduces the concept of the *triple hermeneutic*, borrowing it from B. Protter (1996) but applying it to psychoanalysis as the third hermeneutic task for the analyst: interpreting the particular choice in the analytical situation of those common meanings which have become habitual and for this reason difficult to perceive in the analytical situation in the moment in which the field begins to have its own historical dimension, which renders it absolutely unique. This third level of the mediation of meaning becomes necessary through the consideration that any event of the treatment is deeply rooted in that particular ensemble of prejudices – in the Gadamerian sense – which the patient and the analyst have established in the field.

In summing up: "courting surprise" (Stern, 1997, pp. 235–255) calls for dissolving reciprocal dissociations; the most stubborn dissociation of the enactments are "strong dissociations" (Stern, 1997, pp. 129–145); being a dissociated enactment, it is unformulated and is to be formulated; the state of reciprocal dissociation is an elaboration of the "hold on the field" on the two participants to the analytical field (Stern, 1997, pp. 185–201). The rupture of the dissociation and the subsequent resolution of the enactment are signals that confirm that an attitude of mental openness – that is, curiosity – has been manifested.

> To be curious is to be determined to know what is already there – what one is already aware of being confronted with – in the most detailed and complete way possible. [...] Curiosity means being in the process of differentiating whatever perceptions one has already identified; the unbidden emerges from that which has been meticulously described. [...] To be curious is to be sensitive to the possibility of a question.
>
> (Stern, 1997, pp. 249–250)

> [...] clinical practice does demand a high level of openness. The analyst develops a 'work ego' in the course of treatment and training, a capacity for self-containment and self-reflection, which may originally have been the training analyst's, but is now the analyst's own, and will become the patient's [...] .
>
> (Stern, 1997, p. 254)

Chapter 10

The Psychoanalytic Thought of Edgar Levenson

I only met Edgar Levenson once, in his Manhattan studio. What struck me first was a photograph that was hanging in the waiting room. It captured an older Indian man, with the typical absolutely white turban, tilling the soil and wearing an expression of weariness beneath the searing sun, but at the same time, he looked to be a man of great dignity and composure, which the extensive wrinkles of his face amplified. A kind of peasant-king. What I liked was that it not only portrayed India, an enduring metaphor for the inner journey, but especially the message that anyone could become a person, could acquire dignity, whatever his/her social status.

I wanted to invite him to conduct a seminar at my Institute in Florence, but he didn't like to hold seminars. I recall an extremely kind, welcoming person but someone firm in their beliefs. He tried to make me feel at ease despite my poor English at the time. I am happy to have recently had a brief email exchange with him. I was finally able to tell him how grateful I was for his work and that I taught his ideas in my contemporary interpersonal psychoanalysis course in various schools in Italy and beyond.

He was always a pioneer and original in his thinking.

> Levenson elaborates on the themes that have preoccupied him from the beginning: the creation and development of inter-personal psychoanalysis, the analyst's use of his/her own experience, and most of all, the nature of psychoanalytic process. Levenson is impatient with the imposition of meaning on experience, labeling it 'metapsychology'. He believes that new

DOI: 10.4324/9781003512844-14

meanings, thoughts, and feelings come about unpredictably, and by themselves, once the treatment deconstructs the old patterns and narratives. The creation of instability is Levenson's aim; interpretations designed to create new meanings are less interesting, and certainly less profound. There is no recipe, no theory of technique, for deconstruction. Levenson shows us, and convinces us, that we never know exactly what we are doing, or why whatever we did made the difference it did. Or whether what we did made the difference. Or even what the difference was that we thought the treatment made! Levenson never stands still. The ground is always shifting under his feet, and under ours as we read him. […] Levenson is not only profound, he is also a brilliant literary stylist. And he is funny […] .

(Stern, in Levenson, 2018, p. XI)

Semiotic Confusion and Mental Distress

Levenson was committed to defining the specific, original identity of the interpersonal paradigm by suggesting his own personal vision of the origin of the neurotic disturbance. For him, it was not a case of the tracing back in itself to the real parent, but to the semiotic confusion with which the child is addressed. He proposed different levels of message to be decoded. Thus, the situation becomes strongly pathogenic because it is extremely confusing and disorienting. Basically, for him, the role of mystification lies at the origin of mental suffering.

He thinks that people have difficulty in their lives not so much because they have suffered terrible traumas, but because they are harnessed into a fleeting semiotic story of omissions and falsifications. And so, they cannot generate a semiotic competence that requires a non- equivocal experience in order to develop.

A child, according to Levenson, learns about reality through how it is ordered and organized in language, and in turn he/ she uses language to build his/her reality. Hence incompetence on the linguistic level will compromise not only the ability to understand others, but also the possibility of getting from these others answers that are appropriate and functional for his/her own needs.

(Amadei, 2001, p. 91, my translation)

Mental distress in this way is the consequence, not the cause, of the distorted interpretation of reality.

Levenson is interested in what one does with the patient rather than in creating a metapsychology which would then end in confirming one's own theories in clinical practice. To his mind, this makes psychoanalysis a form of persuasion, not of cure (1983), because the analyst is intent on looking for what he expects to find by following his/her own theoretical references, rather than on listening to what the patient is trying to say.

Following Levenson's thought pattern, if in classical psycho-analysis the figure of the analyst was seen as that of Virgil, who accompanies Dante in Hades, in the interpersonal, the analyst evokes the figure of Leopold Bloom with his Stephen Dedalus in the Joycean masterpiece: the analyst's ability lies above all in the capacity to tolerate uncertainty, impotence and the confusion of staying at length in the fog, the labyrinth, losing him/herself and then again finding him/herself in a new and continuously more intimate relationship with the other.

I think we cure people by tapping into and participating in a largely unconscious – with bubbles of awareness – pro-cess. I think that brain is individual but mind is a field phenomenon, a network, a web. To paraphrase Winnicott's famous 'there's no such thing as a baby'– implying that the mother-child dyad is the indivisible unit – I would say that there is no such thing as a mind. It takes others to extend that network and the extension may be, in itself, restorative. Perhaps the issue is not insight but learning, which involves issues of memory. [...] Memory prefigures learning, which prefigures change.

(Levenson, 2018, p. 248)

The Fallacy of Understanding

He proceeds from the assumption that each psychoanalyst, of any orientation, is able to achieve good results. Therefore, there must be something in the common premise of therapy that is detached from a particular orientation. He thus traced a type of procedure that he called *algorithm*: success does not depend on theoretical correctness. In fact, the paradigm can be mistaken and yet the algorithm can function (Levenson, 2006).

This algorithm can be divided into three stages:

1 Establishing and defining the therapeutic framework, in other words beginning to create the therapeutic setting, the frame, through the definition of a series of contractual rules.
2 Elaborating on and enriching the data relative to the patient's life. Upon expansion of this data, models of experience will begin to emerge – patterns of behavior that are similar and tend to be present in different moments and contexts of the patient's life – a sort of remarkable intrinsic order, an overall coherence in what seemed a total chaos (Levenson, 1983).
3 Using the therapist/patient relationship. For Levenson, too, the dialogical nature of the analytic process presupposes the participation of the analyst. We cannot remain external to what we are observing, and it is never possible to trace a line that clearly and definitively separates what we call "reality" from our observation.

The analytic relationship is for him a semiotic dimension of an isomorphic type: the analyst is also continuously immersed in the continual flow of the process. His interventions are also always *actions* (Levenson, 1983).

Change

Levenson has contributed to the evolution of psychoanalytic thought in relation to the most diverse subjects – the psycho-analytic process, the function of interpretation, the transference/countertransference dynamic – by being open to integrating them with mathematics, neuroscience and systems theory. And he always does so with originality and elegance.

For Levenson, reliving the past is only a metaphor because the real past is not truly available for direct examination. What is described as a revisiting of the past corresponds in reality to the patient's reconstruction of events that are already irrevocably past in order to make present behavior understandable.

So, the conception of memory turns out to be modified because if memories are nothing but systems of symbolic representation that have a great deal to do with the present, then memory is a process similar to the dream, and it, too, is directly proportional to the analyst/patient relationship. Out of this comes a non-static idea of the mind, a processual understanding of psychic development and with it of therapy. In Levenson, the process therefore becomes the true center of psychoanalytic interest (Zito, 2006).

If one can accept that one is tapping into and riding, like a wave, an ineffable process – part conscious, part unconscious, part between people, part autonomous, part rational conceptualizing, and part a mysterious act of mutual creation – then one might wish to augment and facilitate the process without needing to grasp it firmly. [...] I would like to suggest that the act, the praxis of psychoanalysis – the inquiry, association, dreams, fantasies, and the reiteration of those themes in the behavioral field of patient and therapist, in the office and as it extends into their private worlds – is the cure! The medium may indeed be the message. Psychoanalysis is subject to a dialectical rhythm. Every advance is initially productive, turns into a doctrine, and ends as a cliché and a countertransference. Then the next cycle of reversal begins. Intrapsychic and interpersonal exist on just such a dialectic wheel. I believe that after an intense involvement with transferential enactments and their ramifications – and just as traditional psychoanalysts are discovering the interpersonal – many interpersonalists are experiencing a resurgence of interest in the patient's intrapsychic processes. And, by intrapsychic I do not mean what is in the unconscious – for example, the libido theory – but how unconscious mentation works. Because our goal is to effect change in our patients, it behooves us to attend to how people learn and change, the relationship of what is said to what is done, of experience to conceptualization of experience. Otherwise, we shall be left behind, like magicians, muttering our incantations and wondering why the magic does not work.

(Levenson, 2018, pp. 248–249)

Edgar Levenson – one of the greatest masters of change in psychoanalysis.

Chapter 11

Brief References to Other Interpersonal Protagonists and Interpreters of Interpersonalism

This chapter is dedicated to mentioning, albeit briefly, some of the more significant authors who have contributed to the development of contemporary psychoanalysis. They obviously deserve more than this concise summary, but as mentioned in the introduction, it can't be helped.

However, I encourage colleagues and students to read their books and articles because, as I have often stated in this book, all the interpersonal authors possess the gift of clarity. One feels that they truly desire to transmit their ideas, so they do not indulge in complicated constructs if these do not represent a valid support for those who work in this field, while at the same time they never lose depth, acuity and originality. For this reason, I will always be grateful to all of these interpersonal authors.

In the first generation, besides Sullivan and Thompson, we also have Fromm, Fromm-Reichmann, Rioch, Tauber, Shachtel and some others. I will not speak of their work. For whoever is interested, I suggest you consult the text by Stern, Kantor, Mann and Schlesinger (1995), *Pioneers of Interpersonal Psychoanalysis*, which is partly dedicated to the works of the first generation and partly to the second generation of interpersonalists.

In this text, those writers of the second and third generation will not be included, writers such as Walter Bonime, with his study of dreams; Gerard Chrzanowski; Carola Mann, who has applied herself in a major way to the study of the development of interpersonalism outside of the USA (she helped me organize the seminars at the White Institute with my colleagues and students);

DOI: 10.4324/9781003512844-15

Margaret Crastnopol; Richard Gartner, with his studies about sexual abuse in adolescence and about trauma; Alan Grey; Maurice Green, to whom we owe the biography of Clara Thompson, and for his work with Edward Tauber; Elizabeth Howell, with her book on dissociation; Ruth Imber; Jay Kwawer; Marylou Lionells; Paul Lippmann; Jorge Bose, with his interpersonal elaboration of depression; Marcelo Rubin, with his studies on adolescence; Pat Pantone; Ira Moses; Seth Aronson; Elizabeth Hegeman, with her in-depth study of post-traumatic stress disorder; and many others. This exclusion is due to the main theme of this text (see Introduction) and to the limitations of space. In fact, I will restrict myself to speaking in a more specific manner of only a few authors who have pro-vided indispensable contributions to contemporary psycho-analysis, and to whom some I feel connected with a bond of friendship. We owe a great debt to all of them for their origin-ality and the brilliance of their contributions. I will proceed in alphabetical order.

Mark Blechner is well-known for his studies on sexuality and on dreams. It is particularly important to mention his work "Group Dream Interpretation" (2011), an excellent tool for training psy-chotherapists to become familiarized with unconscious commu-nication. His latest book, *The Mindbrain and Dreams* (2018), is also noteworthy. In it he posits the dream as a bridge between psychoanalysis and neuroscience.

Philip Bromberg (1998, 2006, 2011) has been concerned with trauma and dissociative states, reinterpreted within a relational vision of the clinical process and of therapeutic change. He has underlined the central role played by trauma in personality dis-orders, using the Sullivanian concept of dissociation, and estab-lishing their implications for the therapeutic relationship. For Bromberg, the mind and mental functioning are based on a com-plex configuration of changeable states of awareness, each one with its own subjective reality, held in a dynamic interaction of dissociative-type processes. Health, therefore, lies not only in inte-gration but in the capacity of *standing in the spaces* between dif-ferent realities without losing any one of them, to consequently feel *one in many*.

Hilde Bruch is mostly known for her work on eating disorders. Her voice remains to date an indispensable reference for those concerned with these disorders (1973, 1988).

Sandra Buechler is a prolific and impassioned writer, a doyenne of interpersonalism. The first time I met her was at the White Institute in 2005, and since then I have had the good fortune to get to know her better, and to appreciate her ideas, whether pertaining to the profession or not. Her writings have great relevance in interpersonal thought. They focus on analysis deepened by *emotions*, especially those of the therapist, and on the *clinical values* that can truly produce change. She always encourages us to remember that effective clinical work revolves around the ability to draw the maximum from the humanity of the patient and the analyst (1995, 2004, 2008, 2012, 2017). An insightful connoisseur of the philosophy of Erich Fromm, she conducts seminars all over the world on these themes, to which she has recently added her love of poetry, for the emotional resonance that poetry generates in the reader and for its transformative power (2021).

Jack Drescher has been one of the most courageous psycho-analysts to have fought against so-called conversion therapy. He even succeeded in revising the DSM-IV-TR diagnosis of Gender Identity Disorder to the DSM-5 diagnosis of Gender Dysphoria. A psychiatrist and a psychoanalyst who trained at the White Institute, he is especially known for his numerous writings on sexuality, on the diagnosis of gender and on mental health (2015, 2017; Drescher and Byne, 2017). Having met him for the first time in 2005 at the White Institute, I found him to be a warm and amiable person, besides being a skilled teacher. I have invited him several times to Florence, where his seminars are attended with great interest.

Darlene Ehrenberg (1992) has studied in depth the importance of vulnerability to the collusion and enactment of the analyst and patient. She has particularly dealt with how the work process, in terms of the intimacy of the analytic relationship, involves an effort of external and internal work on the analytic (inter)subjectivity.

John Fiscalini (1994, 1995a) has been very dedicated to narcissis-tic-type disorders, integrating Kohut's theory on this matter with the interpersonal approach. He defines narcissism as a Self-disorder which transversally crosses all the different kinds of psychopathological functioning. In other words, he defines narcissism as a type of problem, not as a type of person. Thus, he establishes the relevant parent/child patterns in the development of the narcissistic personality: the humiliated child, the spoiled child and the special child.

Emmanuel Ghent (1990) offers us an original idea on "surrender", studying its relationship with submission and masochism, considered the antithesis of surrender. He delved into the experience of surrendering to connote the subjective experience that corresponds to the "liberation and expansion of the self". The experience of surrendering constitutes the common thread that passes through the treatment of neurosis. Therefore, the term "surrender" has a connotation of defeat but indicates a quality of liberation and expansion of the self as a corollary to the breaking down of defensive barriers.

Jay Greenberg is a Training and Supervising Analyst of the W. A. White Institute. I met Jay Greenberg, and Steve Mitchell too, in 1988, in Florence, where their famous book, *Object Relations in Psychoanalytic Theory* (1983), was being presented for the first time in Italian, becoming a psychoanalytic classic soon after its publication. He later became the first interpersonalist that we decided to invite when I was the president of the Italian Society of Interpersonal Psychoanalysis, in May of 2005 in Florence, for a conference on changes to the concept of the unconscious, a conference that we replicated, at which he was again present, twelve years later, on the same topic, to update how things stood relative to the same concept. My colleagues and I took advantage of the occasion to get him to conduct entire days of classes at the institute, in which we appreciated his clarity and eloquence, besides his ability to always be warm and friendly. Besides the book written with Mitchell, Jay Greenberg is the author of *Oedipus and Beyond* (1991b), in which he argues that all psychoanalytic theories contain a theory of drives, implicitly or explicitly. The concept of drive is therefore essential to him, since without drives man would be like a piece of putty, totally passive, shaped by external social influences (Mitchell, 2000). One of the greatest contemporary theoreticians, he has dealt with and continues to deal with comparative psychoanalysis, the theory of therapeutic action and the development of interpersonal and relational psychoanalysis (1986, 1991a, 2017).

We continue this brief overview with another world-class author who deserves a book unto himself: Harold Searles (1959, 1965, 1979, 1986). His writings represent an indispensable reading of the emotional responses to what takes place in the analytical relationship, and with regard to the courage to open oneself to a receptivity towards the patient's unconscious communications, which necessarily requires an ability for an exploration and a laying bare of the analyst's own unconscious experience.

Benjamin Wolstein (1954, 1959, 1997) had an enormous impact on contemporary clinical psychology, advancing above all the legacy of Clara Thompson, who had been his analyst, on the study of countertransference, a legacy compiled in turn by Irwin Hirsch (chapter 7). Furthermore, what is also relevant is his concept of "unique individuality" as direct experience, along with his view that an experience of "shared individuality" is one of the most therapeutic interpersonal interactions possible in clinical psychoanalysis.

Chapter 12

My Personal Interpersonalism

I am very pleased to have the opportunity to speak about my personal way of living interpersonalism thus far. It has profoundly permeated both my professional field as well as my way of relating to others in general. I have always felt very supported by it, and over time I have increasingly broadened my perspective, enhancing it with the most recent positions of contemporary psychoanalysis and often detecting with amazement how much the thinking of Sullivan and many other interpersonalists have been ground-breaking and innovative.

And now I will express my reasoning for these assertions.

How interpersonal psychoanalysis has mostly helped me and the fact that it constantly accompanies me in my clinical work pertains especially to the theoretical frame, in which dissociation assumes a unique significance, and it is also relevant to the way in which I allow myself today to use my subjectivity in the service of the clinical process.

I believe that what made me inclined to delve deeper into interpersonal theory and clinical practice is deeply immersed in the libertarian and antidogmatic spirit which right from the beginning characterized this current of thought. The courage to dare to open oneself up to new perspectives and the breadth of views of the pioneers of this approach has been for me a beacon which has attracted and directed me over the course of my work, and still continues to do so.

Besides this, the connection to some of its contemporary representatives has reinforced my sense of belonging, in that I have

DOI: 10.4324/9781003512844-16

always continued to see in them the same scientific curiosity, the same freedom to dare, and at the same time the same straightforwardness in going directly to the point which I had ascertained when studying the first interpersonalists – in other words, all those fundamental clinical values in this tradition, which to me seem essential for being within the analytical relationship and within relationships in general.

The analyst that recognizes him/herself in this approach embraces moral and ethical values such as hope, courage, trust, the sense of having a goal, the willingness to collaborate, sincerity, the ability to be intimate, the use of emotions as crucial elements of the treatment (Buechler, 2004, 2008).

If we have to help the other to be capable of intimacy in a relationship, it is indisputable that we should be the first to facilitate it and *witness it* as much as possible and be able to enjoy it as a precious gift. Only in this way do we become genuine companions on the experiential journey, and by abandoning every ambition to be life masters. We do not know how the other will be able to express best his subjectivity and enjoy it, but we can search together with him/her the way in which he/she will be able to express it best.

In fact, intimacy as a therapeutic factor has nothing to do with the simple reaching of a generic intimacy with the patient, but rather with not backing down in terms of analyzing and confronting the various affective states and the different psychic personifications that surface over the course of treatment, no matter how uncomfortable, threatening and unexpected these may be.

Now I will try to briefly expound upon my way of living interpersonalism to date. I will speak about *my* way – that is, what *I* do and how *I* do it. And I will try to show you this by means of several vignettes. From the commentary on these vignettes, my personal anchoring to interpersonalism will easily become clear.

As already stated, the direct unembellished style of interpersonal thinkers has constituted for me a valuable heritage.

I trained as a psychoanalyst in the seventies, years in which many were used to analyzing by exercising authority and distance. My first training began in 1978 at the Istituto di Psicoterapia Analitica di Firenze (The Institute for Analytical Psychotherapy of Florence), where today I am Training and Supervising analyst and teacher of two courses on Interpersonal Psychoanalysis. At that time, it was an institute, in a certain sense, dedicated to pluralism: analyses were conducted there and analysts taught there, all representing different approaches. There were Jungians, Freudians, Kleinians and even Frommians, given that at that time Fromm's thinking had penetrated for quite some time the Italian psychoanalytical cultural fabric. This picture could seem positive, but in reality, I left there very confused, without a psychoanalytical identity with a coherent basis, with many implicit theories that my mind did not even distinguish.

In 1988, I had the good fortune to meet and hear Jay Greenberg and Steven Mitchell in Florence, invited for the first time to Italy by our Institute, and thus I came into contact with their fundamental text *Object Relations in Psychoanalytic Theory* (1983), which had just been published in Italian. Immediately afterwards, a reading of Thompson's text *Interpersonal Psychoanalysis*, also just translated into Italian, gave voice to many ideas, thoughts and doubts that were lodged inside of me, and I decided that I wished to dig deeper into this approach that was so original and at the same time so courageous, in an era in which themes such as neutrality were still considered fundamental. I also had the good fortune to share this passion with the colleagues with whom I had trained, companions on a journey of more than four decades now. In 1991 we became a Member Society of the International Federation of Psychoanalytic Societies (IFPS), of which I have the honor of being the Secretary General since October 2024. In 1996, we became also a Member Society of OPIFER, which is the most important Confederation of Italian Relational Societies.

In 2000, I began a second course of training, which lasted for a long time, with Pier Francesco Galli, who was very close to Sullivan's and Fromm's way of thinking. He, the father of relational and interpersonal psychoanalysis in Italy, recently deceased, had in fact succeeded in getting all of their works translated. Otherwise, these works would not have been accessible at the time, at least not in Italy. This, I think, is one of the reasons for which interpersonalism is little or not well known by most people.

Embracing and employing the interpersonal analytical dimension brought with it for me a greater commitment within sessions with patients. It is in fact very tiring to let oneself be involved with and feel safe behind an alleged neutrality, and behind the fact that one has been analyzed, or behind a rigid use of categorical diagnosis, derived from psychiatry; in short, all those certainties that were in vogue during my first course of training, and which attested to the need for a defensive modality on the part of the analyst. I remember Darlene Ehrenberg, in Florence at one time, in the living room of an old and then famous psychoanalyst in line with the classical mainstream, who insisted a great deal on this point: participating while listening and constantly monitoring one's own feelings, thoughts, experiences, sensations, etc. – as the interpersonalists do – is much more tiring.

Returning to the precious heritage of interpersonalism to which I am indebted, I must add that it has also been naturally helped by other dimensions belonging to contemporary psychoanalysis that I have slowly and steadily come to know during my studies. In fact, by becoming enriched by contributions stemming from other scientific approaches and from other disciplines, like the neurosciences, sociology, the sciences of group and community organizations, the studies on neo-natality, and humanistic approaches, such as philosophy, literature and art in general, contemporary psychoanalysis is above all interested in what has not been represented and integrated into the mind. Its attention therefore addresses how to be able to recover, represent, transform and integrate these types of experiences, in which the bodily experience has come to assume a central role.

In essence, it is about paying attention to the same coordinates that had motivated Sullivan's study (we must recall that his studies started from the desire to understand and heal schizophrenia) and that of the first interpersonalists, for the better understanding and treatment of dissociated experiences that we today would say stem from embodied and non-symbolized experiences.

The interest in and the study of this type of experience has implied an interest in and a deeper study of the bodily experience, which has come to assume an increasingly central role, principally since the sad events linked to Coronavirus (Loiacono, 2023).

Through the input of the neurosciences in the understanding of the mechanisms of the mind/brain/memory functioning, we currently think of intersubjective communication as embodied cognition (Panksepp, 2009; Schore, 2003; Stern, 2004). Thus, the mind is embodied (Damasio, 2006), and we speak of "embodied cognitive science" (Wilson and Foglia, 2011, paragraph 1). This genre of study (Lombardi, 2002; Lemma, 2015) has helped me to be more flexible and accepting towards emotions which originate in the body, making me, at least so I believe, even more able to grasp the so to speak "poetic" aspects intrinsic to the clinical process, something already stimulated by interpersonalism.

I believe that for me this is equivalent to feeling better able to enter into contact with that prototaxic dimension of experience that Sullivan, in a totally autonomous way, had come to theorize (chapter 3). Allowing myself to perceive and letting myself be engaged with that primitive or in fact prototaxic sensoriality, with which one enters into contact in the therapeutic relationship, allows me to already feel in the body all the difficulties of the building of *the Self with the other*, about which Sullivan speaks to us (1953).

On this subject, let us recall the already cited example of the luminous image,

> in which for each experience it is as if someone turned on a light bulb, and this constitutes a basic prototaxic experience. This mode of experience therefore constitutes a creative act, an artistic act as well as a unique one, in that the flow which enters ignites specific light bulbs and not others, which would be turned on if the 'group of two' were made up of other people.
>
> (chapter 3)

I have defined this artistic act as the *"poetics of the symptom"* (Loiacono, 2024).

I hope that the presentation of the following clinical case will prove explanatory with regard to the way in which I live the analytical process.

Clinical Case

The following clinical case has been taken from my article "The Poetics of the Symptom" (Loiacono, 2024).

Marinella comes to see me because of severe attacks of jealousy towards her husband, who has threatened to leave her if the violent intensity of her outbursts together with the controlling stranglehold she subjects him to do not abate. She complains about no longer being able to trust him, about the fact that he had in effect betrayed her at the start of their relationship. It is also noteworthy to add that Marinella was constantly cheating on her husband, feeling she had the right to do this because of the stinging disillusionment she had suffered early on in their relationship.

By working on her internal process, what emerged were also the parental personifications living within her. Both her mother and father belonged to that Italian petit bourgeoisie that had easily grown rich through business during the economic boom of the sixties and seventies and had achieved more than considerable financial stability. Uncultured, these parents shared a passion for leisure, social life and travel. Marinella, an only child, quickly learned that her father was quite a philanderer, and her mother, inconsistent, depressed and focused on herself, used her to help spy on and monitor the sexual escapades of her father, including following him in the middle of the night, ventures that unfailingly revealed his betrayal in action. Her father was hyper-stimulating and abusive: he had wanted a male child, and during her childhood he had treated her like a boy, often playing with her but also even teaching her to drive a tractor at seven years of age. Not only did he involve her from a young age in his dalliances, requesting her to cover for him with her mother, but as soon as she became of age he began to have affairs with almost all of her best friends. The most striking of all these situations that Marinella remembers is the month-long holiday they spent on her father's boat, during which her father was together with her best friend, and Marinella was together with her father's best friend, someone equal in age to him.

What emerges, therefore, are two empathetic and non-mirroring figures – her mother and father – with whom pre-oedipal and oedipal matters were experienced in an extremely traumatic manner.

The parents separated immediately after Marinella went to live on her own. Obviously, she played a role in keeping her parents together. As soon as she left, the parents also left each other.

In her relationship with me, after a lengthy period in which the relationship was extremely fusional, in which I felt that the setting was adopting the function of being a specific "skin" to the so-called "embodied setting" (Civitarese, 2008; Lemma, 2015), I began to feel that I was, dangerously, but inevitably, colluding with her desire for omnipotent control, by accepting the roles that little by little she was imposing upon me, and rationalizing my submission as a way to assuage her overlooked developmental needs (Greenberg, 2017). Her umpteenth unannounced late arrival, in a moment in which she had triangulated our relationship through her relationship with a man "of my age" – an act which demonstrated the pre-oedipal and oedipal problems which we were going through, and therefore an exit from fusionality, a beginning of separation – elicited in me a kind of rebellion against the corner into which she had lured me, in which I was feeling as if I had allowed my otherness to be slowly denied to the point where it could only occupy the tiniest of spaces. I thus related to her my experiences, in an intensely heartfelt exchange, but one which also contained a paralyzing aggressivity, as if she had caught me in a net, in which, if I disregarded what she was asking me, she would have felt betrayed, unloved and corroborated in her violent frenzied pain of not being able to abandon herself to love, of being able to experience only distrust towards the other.

A deadly trap, for her and for me.

After several more or less silent exchanges, she was reminded of her grasshopper phobia. She had worked on this symptom long before turning to me, through hypnosis, from which she had derived a certain amount of benefit, but still merely the thought of a grasshopper's body, with its "little hooks that stick to each other like suction cups and make that typical cla cla cla chirping sound …", makes her shiver.

After a long process, it subsequently emerged that grasshoppers effectively represented the concretization of the jealousy and abuse – that is, the hyper-stimulation and the seduction which she suffered at the hands of both parents and which Marinella re-actualized in her relationship with her husband, as well as with me.

Thus, these insects form a sort of sensorial concentrate, one which also encloses within it those experiences of incestuous seduction that significantly traumatized her. The grasshopper's body condenses all the sensoriality of the sticky tenacious relationship with her mother (the suction-like hooks), characterized by the ambiguity of the love bond, where to love means to possess, where the narcissistic space dictates a negation of alterity. It also contains the entire ambiguity of the relationship with her father, at first filled with negation – he wanted a boy and treated her like one – and then incestuousness, once she was acknowledged as a girl, where again the other becomes trapped in a perverse desire, without an escape route – I love you and I desire you, but we will never be together.

What inevitably transpires for Marinella is a terminal-type relationship with the object (Bollas, 1995), exactly as in the symbol of the grasshoppers: only distrust towards positive emotions, the need to not believe, not surrender to the love of the other allows her to feel a sense of internal coherence; it organizes her; it gives her a purpose, namely that of "uncovering the betrayal of the other". It was here that my experiences of submission and impotence sunk their roots, as well as my feeling of being entrapped.

This reminds me of Thomas Ogden, when he wrote:

> The rejecting object and the internal saboteur are determined to nurse their feelings of having been deeply wronged, cheated, humiliated, betrayed, exploited, treated unfairly, discriminated against, and so on. The mistreatment at the hands of the other is felt to be unforgivable. An apology is forever expected by each, but never offered by either. Nothing is more important to the internal saboteur (the rejected self) than coercing the rejecting object into recognizing the incalculable pain that he or she has caused.
>
> (Ogden, 2010, p. 109)

Repression of the pain and sorrow she felt due to her parents' behaviors and her husband's infidelities had given rise to a desire for revenge, a desire which psychologically kept her captive, aiming her life above all towards "making him pay" for her wounded pride (Horney, 1950; Kohut, 1978; Searles, 1965).

At the same time, both the grasshopper phobia and the excessive jealousy towards her husband lent themselves to containing and maintaining important original sensory experiences, and to preserving the underlying love bond – even if one of disappointment – with her parents, offering the perception of a maintenance of that connection with the traumatic figures, and, at the same time, ensuring avoidance of contact with the experiences associated with them.

In short, the sticky suction pads, the antennae, the eyes, the leathery body, all of which in some way can contain sensorial experiences of another kind – for example, relational experiences with her mother and father and various objects – also represent a sort of poetics, even if tragic until giving voice to it, understood in the sense of an implicit and concretized conception in a sensorial concentrate of a series of markings or traces, which, at any rate, outline a possible depiction of a history. For this person, it was the best modality through which she was able to remain whole in her suffering, containing and carrying her own traumatic issues within herself.

In this case, the verbal expression of the affective experience has been blocked in order to protect an indispensable bond, so one of the main tasks is to investigate what emerges within the transference-countertransference matrix of the relationship. In some way the patient expects and fears that his/her emerging emotions will receive the same pathogenic responses from the analyst as he/she had received in the original environment. In the relationship with Marinella, I maintain that an important aspect was redressed by my style of listening, by the sensorial and emotional resonances, by the thoughts and fantasies shared within the relational field, in which it was possible to allow the "unformulated" side of her experience to emerge and then be decoded (Stern, 1997).

The grasshopper thus comes to represent a sensorial condensation of data, enclosing important original sensorial experiences of the relationship with her parents and other objects that have been hallucinated within it; a sort of poetics that allowed her to stay in contact with traumatic figures, without being submerged in the sensoriality of traumatic experiences (Loiacono, 2024).

Change and the Use of the Analyst's Subjectivity

In continuing to briefly present my debt to interpersonalism, I will add that I owe to my personal interpretation of it the belief that my function as therapist for the purpose of producing change is that of seeking to expand the transformative space of people, not that of healing them, which would mean removing them from memory. This action occurs both through verbal language and through action as a type of overall presence (a concept of the semantics of action with respect to language as an interpretive function).

Change is generated through the subtleties in the way in which the analyst is with the patient, independently from the rituals and interpretive conventions of any evolutive theory or theory of therapeutic action (Levenson, 2018). It depends on how and how much the therapist him/herself is ready to tolerate surprise for what happens spontaneously (*even court surprise*, in the language of D. B. Stern (1997)).

Consider this vignette:

S. is in her seventh year of analysis on a biweekly basis. The session in question flows calmly, cheerfully and is full of freshness. After all this vitality, at the end of the session, S. says to me: 'And yet, there is something strange that I want to tell you, that is to say, all this life … and yet, I feel that there is something instead … I can't use any other word but *loss.* I feel a strong sense of loss.' In that moment, while she is saying these words to me, I have the sensation that she has stood up and physically withdrawn but left a dead shadow on the couch, and she adds: 'It is as if a part of me is dying'. 'Yes, so it is'. I corroborate her statement, referring to her change: she is truly witnessing the reality of how much she has changed, of how much her life and she herself has changed. 'But it's painful. I feel that I can't do anything else. It is as if a current is pushing me, and I am *happy* to follow this current.' Thus S. ends her discourse, expressing in the best of ways the essence of the psychoanalytic process with regard to change.

I felt that I could share with her this new and spontaneous experience, co-created in our interaction, in our embodied relationship. Don Stern (2015, 2024) tells us that spontaneous experience hits our mind and our body spontaneously and suddenly, springing out of nowhere.

Experience simply *is* (we recall Gadamer, chapter 6) and confers an emotional and cognitively tangible form to what we are living. Therefore, the spontaneous lies at the heart of therapeutic action and is at the same time the nucleus of the process of change and the indicator which we consult to evaluate such change (Stern, 2015).

Embracing and accepting new experiences thus becomes the principal way of defining a person's health. Sullivan (1953) in fact had attested that psychic health consists in drawing benefit from new experiences, whatever they may be. Sandra Buechler (2004, 2008, 2012), for her part, on this matter, has presented us with the most profound and poetic definition: it consists of the capacity to *forgive* life, given the inevitability of its tragic nature.

This brings to mind the vision of Nietzsche's tragic man, a constant builder of sandcastles without paying heed to the arrival of the tides. In essence, it means being in tune with suffering – allowing ourselves to be permeated by it whilst managing not to lose hope because we know that we have the values that help us and direct us in our work.

Conclusion

I wish to end this book with a poetic image, hoping to reach the reader in the best possible way, having aroused his/her curiosity and perhaps indeed inspired him/her. This is an excerpt taken from a book by Fred Vargas, an extraordinary writer of detective novels. By means of a description of the mind of the protagonist, commissaire Adamsberg, the author grasps the essence of what is for me, at present, the best method for employing my subjectivity in the service of change; it synthesizes what lies at the heart of my interpersonalism in my professional practice and in my life:

let his thoughts wander as they would without trying to organize them. He had recently seen a photograph that had struck him as a clear illustration of his own idea of his brain. It showed the contents of a fishing net unloaded on the deck of a large vessel, a pile taller than the fishermen themselves, a heap of all kinds of things defying identification, in which the silvery colors of the fish mingled with the dark brown of seaweed, the grey of the crustaceans – marine ones, not that damned woodlouse – the blue of lobsters, the white of seashells, making it hard to distinguish the different elements. That was what he was always fighting, the confused, multiform and shifting mass, always ready to change or vanish, and float off again into the sea. The sailors were sorting out the pile, throwing back creatures that were too small, lumps of seaweed or detritus, and saving the familiar useful species. Adamsberg, it seemed to him, did the opposite, throwing out all the sensible items and then looking at the irrelevant fragments of his personal collection.

(Vargas, 2014, pp. 322–323)

References

Albarella, C., and Donadio, M. (eds). (1998). *Il Controtransfert* [Countertransference]. Naples: Liguori Editore.

Albasi, C. (2006). *Attaccamenti traumatici*. Rome: Utet.

Alexander, F., and French, T.M.*et al.* (1946). *Psychoanalytic Therapy: Principles and Application*. New York: Ronald Press.

Amadei, G. (2001). *Il paradigma celato* [The Hidden Paradigm]. Milan: Unicopli.

Ancona, L. (1972). L'aspetto dinamico della motivazione, il conflitto psichico e i meccanismi di difesa [The Dynamic Aspect of Motivation, the Psychic Conflict and the Defensive Mechanisms]. In *Nuove Questioni di Psicologia* [New Issues in Psychology] Vol. I (ch. 21, pp. 887–919). Brescia: La Scuola.

Benedetti, G. (1961). *Prefazione all'edizione italiana* [Preface to the Italian Edition]. In H.S. Sullivan, *La moderna concezione della psichiatria* [Conceptions of Modern Psychiatry] (pp. VII–XXVII). Milan: Feltrinelli.

Benjamin, J. (2017). *Intersubjectivity and the Third*. London: Routledge.

Blechner, M.J. (2009). The Gay Harry Stack Sullivan: Interactions between His Life, Clinical Work, and Theory. In *Sex Changes* (ch.10, pp. 105–132). New York: Routledge.

Blechner, M.J. (2011). Group dream interpretation. *Contemp. Psychoanal.*, 47(3): 406–419. doi:10.1080/00107530.2011.10746466.

Blechner, M.J. (2018). *The Mindbrain and Dreams*. London: Routledge.

Bleger, J. (1967). Psycho-analysis of the Psycho-analytic Setting. In J. Churcher and L. Bleger (eds), *Symbiosis and Ambiguity: A Psychoanalytic Study*. London: Routledge.

Bollas, C. (1983). Expressive uses of countertransference. *Contemp. Psychoanal.*, 19: 1–34.

Bollas, C. (1995). *Cracking Up: The Work of Unconscious Experience.* New York: Hill and Wang.

Bromberg, P. (1998/2001). *Standing in the Spaces: Essays on Clinical Process, Trauma, and Dissociation.* Hillsdale, NJ: Analytic Press.

Bromberg, P. (2006). *Awakening the Dreamer: Clinical Journeys.* Hillsdale, NJ: Analytic Press.

Bromberg, P. (2011). *The Shadow of the Tsunami and the Growth of the Relational Mind.* New York: Routledge.

Bruch, H. (1973). *Eating Disorders.* New York: Basic Books.

Bruch, H. (1988). *Conversations with Anorexics.* New York: Basic Books.

Buber, M. (1984). *Das Dialogische Prinzip* [The Dialogic Principle]. Heidelberg: Lambert Schneider.

Bucci, W. (2021). *Emotional Communication and Therapeutic Change: Understanding Psychotherapy through Multiple Code Theory.* London: Routledge.

Buechler, S. (1995). Emotion. In D.B. Stern, M. Lionells, J. Fiscalini and C. Mann (eds), *Handbook of Interpersonal Psychoanalysis* (pp. 165–188). Hillsdale, NJ: The Analytic Press.

Buechler, S. (2004). *Clinical Values.* Hillsdale, NJ: The Analytic Press.

Buechler, S. (2008). *Making a Difference in Patients' Lives.* New York: Routledge.

Buechler, S. (2012). *Still Practicing.* New York: Routledge.

Buechler, S. (2017). *Psychoanalytic Reflections: Training and Practice.* New York: International Psychoanalytic Books.

Buechler, S. (2021). *Poetic Dialogues.* Queens, NY: IPBooks.

Civitarese, G. (2008). *L'intima stanza: Teoria e tecnica del campo analitico* [The Intimate Room: Analytic Field's Theory and Technique]. Turin: Borla.

Conci, M. (2000/2012). *Sullivan Revisited: Life and Work.* Trento: Tangram. [Sullivan rivisitato. Bolsena: Massari].

Cooper, S. (1998). Analyst subjectivity, analyst disclosure, and the aims of psychoanalysis. *Psychoanal. Quarterly,* LXVII: 379–406.

Damasio, A. (2006). *Descartes' Error: Emotion, Reason and the Human Brain.* New York: Vintage.

Davies, J.M. (1996). Linking the "pre-analytic" with the postclassical: Integration, dissociation, and the multiplicity of unconscious process. *Contemp. Psychoanal.,* 32(4): 553–576.

Deutsch, H. (1942). Some forms of emotional disturbance and their relationship to schizophrenia. *Psychoanal. Quarterly,* 11: 301–321.

Dottori, R. (1991). Hans Georg Gadamer. In *Novecento Filosofico e Scientifico: Protagonisti* vol 2. [Philosophical and Scientific Twentieth Century: Protagonists] (pp. 407–442). Milan: Marzorati.

Drescher, J. (2015). Queer diagnoses revisited: The past and future of homosexuality and gender diagnoses in DSM and ICD. *International Review of Psychiatry*, 27(5): 386–395.

Drescher, J. (2017). Trauma and Psychoanalysis: Hierarchies of Suffering. In J. Petrucelli and S. Schoen (eds), *The Unknowable, the Unspeakable, and the Unsprung: Psychoanalytic Perspectives on Truth, Scandal, Secrets and Lies* (pp. 61–68). New York and London: Routledge.

Drescher, J., and W. Byne. (2017). Homosexuality, Gay and Lesbian Identities, and Homosexual Behavior. In B.J. Sadock, V.A. Sadock and P. Ruiz (eds), *Kaplan and Sadock's Comprehensive Textbook of Psychiatry, Tenth Edition* (pp. 1982–2013). Philadelphia, PA: Wolters Kluwer.

Eagle, M.N. (2011). *From Classical to Contemporary Psychoanalysis.* London: Taylor & Francis.

Ehrenberg, D. (1992). *The Intimate Edge.* New York: W.W. Norton.

Ehrenberg, D. (1995). Self-disclosure: Therapeutic tool or indulgence? Countertransference disclosure. *Contemp. Psychoanal.*, 31: 213–228.

Feiner, A. H. (1977). Countertransference and the anxiety of influence. *Contemp. Psychoanal.*, 13: 1–16.

Feiner, A. (1991). The analyst's participation in the patient's transference. *Contemp. Psychoanal.*, 27: 208–241.

Fingarette, H. (1963). *The Self in Transformation.* New York: Harper and Row.

Fingarette, H. (1969). *Self-deception.* New York: Humanities Press.

Fiscalini, J. (1994). The uniquely interpersonal and the interpersonally unique. *Contemp. Psychoanal.*, 30(1): 114–134.

Fiscalini, J. (1995a). Narcissism and Self-disorder. In *Handbook of Interpersonal Psychoanalysis* (ch. 15, pp. 333–374). New York: The Analytic Press.

Fiscalini, J. (1995b). Transference and Countertransference. In *Handbook of Interpersonal Psychoanalysis* (ch. 26, pp. 603–616). New York: The Analytic Press.

Freud, S. (1910). *The Future Prospects of Psychoanalytic Therapy.* In Collected Papers, vol. 2 (pp. 285–296). London: The Hogarth Press and The Institute of Psycho-analysis, 5th edition, 1948.

Gadamer, H.G. (1960). *Wahreheit und Methode.* Tübingen: J.C.B. Mohr.

Ghent, E. (1990). Masochism, submission, surrender—Masochism as a perversion of surrender. *Contemp. Psychoanal.*, 26: 108–136.

Giddens, A. (1976). *New Rules of Sociological Method*. New York: Basic Books.

Gill, M. (1983). The interpersonal paradigm and the degree of the therapist's involvement. *Contemp. Psychoanal.*, 19: 200–237.

Green, M.R. (1964). *Interpersonal Psychoanalysis: The Selected Papers of Clara M. Thompson*. New York: Basic Books.

Greenberg, J. (1986). Theoretical models and the analyst's neutrality. *Contemp. Psychoanal.*, 22(1): 87–106.

Greenberg, J. (1991a). Countertransference and reality. *Psychoanal. Dial.*, 1: 52–73.

Greenberg, J. (1991b). *Oedipus and Beyond: A Clinical Theory*. Cambridge, MA: Harvard University Press.

Greenberg, J. (2017). *The Intersubjective Unconscious*. Paper presented at the congress "Prospettive attuali sull'inconscio: Dieci anni dopo" [Current Perspective on the Unconscious: Ten Years Later], held by the Società Italiana di Psicoanalisi Interpersonale [Italian Interpersonal Society of Psychoanalysis – SIPI]. Firenze (Italy), April 22, 2017.

Greenberg, J., and Mitchell, S. (1983). *Object Relations in Psychoanalytic Theory*. Cambridge, MA: Harvard University Press.

Greenberg, J. (1992). *I Never Promised You a Rose Garden*. London: Penguin.

Hegel, G.W.F. (1807). *Phänomenologie des Geistes* [Phenomenology of Spirit]. Erstdruck: Bamberg und Würzburg (Goebhardt).

Heimann, P. (1950). On counter-transference. *Int. J. Psychoanal.*, 31: 81–84.

Heisenberg, W. (1927). Ueber die Grundprincipien der 'Quantenmechanik'. *Forschungen und Fortschritte*, 3: 83.

Hirsch, I. (1990). Countertransference and participant observation. *Amer. J. Psychoanal.*, 50: 275–284.

Hirsch, I. (1995). Therapeutic Uses of Countertransference. In *Handbook of Interpersonal Psychoanalysis* (pp. 643–660). Hillsdale, NJ: The Analytic Press.

Hirsch, I. (1996). Observing-participation, mutual enactment, and the new classical model. *Contemp. Psychoanal.*, 3: 359–383.

Hirsch, I. (1998). The concept of enactment and theoretical convergence. *Psychoanal. Quarterly*, 67: 78–101.

Hirsch, I. (2008). *Coasting in the Countertransference*. New York: Analytic Press.

Hirsch, I. (2015). *The Interpersonal Tradition: The Origins of Psychoanalytic Subjectivity*. New York: Routledge.

Horney, K. (1950). *Neurosis and Human Growth*. New York: W.W. Norton.

Howell, E.F. (2005). *The Dissociative Mind*. London: Taylor & Francis.

Jacoby, R. (1983). *The Repression of Psychoanalysis*. New York: Basic Books.

Janet, P. (1889/2005). *L'automatisme psychologique* [The Psychological Automatism]. Paris: L'Harmattan.

Khan, M.M.R. (1971). "To Hear with Eyes". In *The Privacy of the Self* (pp. 294–306). London: Hogarth Press.

Kohut, H. (1971). *The Analysis of the Self*. London: Hogarth Press.

Kohut, H. (1978). *The Search for the Self*. New York: International University Press.

Korzybski, A. (1921). *Manhood of Humanity: The Science and Art of Human Engineering*. New York: EP Dutton & Co.

Korzybski, A. (1924). *Time-Binding: The General Theory*. New York: EP Dutton & Co.

Kurzweil, E. (1989). *The Freudians: A Comparative Perspective*. New Haven, CT: Yale University Press.

Laplanche, J., and Pontalis, J.B. (1974). *Enciclopedia della psicoanalisi* [Encyclopedia of Psychoanalysis], vol. II. Rome: Laterza.

Lemma, A. (2015). *Minding the Body: The Body in Psychoanalysis and Beyond*. London: Routledge.

Levenson, E. (1972). *The Fallacy of Understanding*. New York: Basic Books.

Levenson, E. (1983). *The Ambiguity of Change*. Northvale, NJ: Jason Aronson.

Levenson, E. (1996). Aspects of self-revelation and self-disclosure. *Contemp. Psychoanal.*, 32(2): 237–248.

Levenson, E. (2006). *Psicoanalisi Contemporanea* (Contemporary Psychoanalysis). R. De Ponte-Conti and S. Caverni (eds). Urbino: QuattroVenti.

Levenson, E. (2018). *Interpersonal Psychoanalysis and the Enigma of Consciousness*. London: Routledge.

Lewin, K. (1935). *A Dynamic Theory of Personality*. New York: McGraw-Hill.

Lewin, K. (1951). *Field Theory in Social Science*. New York: Harper and Brothers.

Loiacono, A.M. (2010). Identità globale: quale futuro? (Global identity: What's the future for it?). *Costruzioni Psicoanalitiche*, 1: 54–65.

Loiacono, A.M. (2016). *La teoria interpersonale di H.S: Sullivan e la clinica della dissociazione* [The Interpersonal Theory of H.S. Sullivan and the Clinic of Dissociation]. Genova: Termanini.

Loiacono, A.M. (2019). Integrating the dissociated: From the dominance of fear to the power of angst – Angst as a 'presence of feeling'. *Intern. Forum of Psychoanal.*, 29(3): 136–141.

Loiacono, A.M. (2021). The problems and contradictions inherent in analytic training and the ultimate requirement: Working with uncertainty. *Amer. J. Psychoanal.*, 81(1), 51–59.

Loiacono, A.M. (2023). Psychoanalysis in the time of coronavirus. *Intern. Forum of Psychoanal.*, 32(4): 247–255.

Loiacono, A.M. (2024). The poetics of the symptom. *Intern. Forum of Psychoanal.*, 33(4): 24–33, copyright © 2024 The International Federation of Psychoanalytic Societies, reprinted by permission of Taylor & Francis Ltd, https://www.tandfonline.com on behalf of The International Federation of Psychoanalytic Societies.

Lombardi, R. (2002). Primitive mental states and the body: A personal view of Armando B. Ferrari's Concrete Original Object. *Int. J. Psychoanal.*, 83: 363–381.

Mitchell, S. (2000). *Relationality: From Attachment to Intersubjectivity.* Hillsdale, NJ: The Analytic Press.

Moore, T.V. (1921). The parataxes: A study and analysis of certain borderline mental states. *Psychoanal. Rev.*, 8: 252.

Ogden, T. (2010). Why read Fairbairn? *Int. J. Psychoanal.*, 91(1): 101–118.

Panksepp, J. (2009). Brain Emotional Systems and Qualities of Mental Life: From Animal Models of Affect to Implications for Psychotherapeutics. In D. Fosha, D.J. Siegel and M.F. Solomon (eds), *The Healing Power of Emotion: Affective Neuroscience, Development & Clinical Practice* (pp. 1–26). New York: W.W. Norton.

Perry, H.S. (1982). *Psychiatrist of America: The Life of Harry Stack Sullivan.* Cambridge, MA and London: The Belknap Press of Harvard University.

Protter, B. (1996). Classical, modern, and postmodern psychoanalysis: Epistemic transformations. *Psychoanal. Dial.*, 6: 533–562.

Putnam, F.W. (1997). *Dissociation in Children and Adolescents.* New York: Guilford Press.

Racker, H. (1968). *Transference and Countertransference.* London: The Hogarth Press and The Institute of Psycho-analysis.

Reik, T. (1948). *Listening with the Third Ear: The Inner Experience of a Psychoanalyst.* New York: Farrar, Straus, & Giroux.

Renik, O. (1999). Playing one's cards face up in analysis: An approach to the problem of self-disclosure. *Psychoanal. Quarterly*, LXVIII: 521–539.

Rychlak, J.F. (1973). An "American" Psychology: The Interpersonal Theory of Harry Stack Sullivan. In *Introduction to Personality and Psychotherapy* (Ch. 5, pp. 323–376). Boston, MA: Houghton Mifflin.

Schore, A.N. (2003). *Affect Regulation and the Repair of the Self.* New York: W.W. Norton.

Searles, H.F. (1959). Oedipal love in the counter transference. *Int. J. Psycho-Anal.*, 40: 180–190.

Searles, H.F. (1965). *Collected Papers on Schizophrenia and Related Objects.* New York: International University Press.

Searles, H.F. (1979). *Countertransference and Related Objects.* New York: International University Press.

Searles, H.F. (1986). *My Work with Borderline Patients.* Northvale, NJ: Jason Aronson.

Shapiro, S.E. (1993). Clara Thompson: Ferenczi's Messenger with Half a Message. In *The Legacy of Sandor Ferenczi* (pp. 159–174). London: Routledge.

Silver, A.L. (1997). Chestnut lodge, then and now. *Contemp. Psychoanal.*, 2: 227–249.

Spiegel, D. (1990). Hypnosis, Dissociation, and Trauma: Hidden and Overt Observers. In J.L. Singer (ed.), *Repression and Dissociation: Implications for Personality Theory, Psychopathology, and Health* (pp. 121–142). Chicago: University of Chicago Press.

Stern, D. (2004). *The Present Moment in Psychotherapy and Everyday Life.* New York: W. W. Norton.

Stern, D.B. (1989). The analyst's unformulated experience of the patient. *Contemp. Psychoanal.*, 19: 71–99.

Stern, D.B. (1997/2003). *Unformulated Experience.* Hillsdale, NJ: Analytic Press.

Stern, D.B. (2002). Words and wordlessness in the psychoanalytic situation. *J. Amer. Psychoanal. Assoc.*, 50: 221–247.

Stern, D.B. (2010). *Partners in Thought: Working with Unformulated Experience, Dissociation, and Enactment.* New York: Routledge.

Stern, D.B. (2013). Relational freedom and therapeutic action. *J. Amer. Psychoanal. Assoc.*, 61: 227–255.

Stern, D.B. (2015). *Relational Freedom: Emergent Properties of the Interpersonal Field.* New York: Routledge.

Stern, D.B. (2019). *The Infinity of the Unsaid.* New York: Routledge.

Stern, D.B. (2024). Beginning the treatment on a personal note: creating emotional connection. *The Psychoanal. Quarterly*, 93(4): 647–674. doi:10.1080/00332828.2024.2398590.

Stern, D.B., and Hirsch, I. (2017). *The Interpersonal Perspective in Psychoanalysis: 1960s-1990s.* New York: Routledge.

Stern, D.B., Kantor, S., Mann, C., and Schlesinger, G. (1995). *Pioneers of Interpersonal Psychoanalysis.* Hillsdale, NJ: The Analytic Press.

Stolorow, R.D., and Atwood, G.E. (1992). *Contexts of Being: The Intersubjective Foundations of Psychological Life.* Hillsdale, NJ: The Analytic Press.

Sullivan, H.S. (1938). Introduction to the study of interpersonal relations. *Psychiatry*, I.

Sullivan, H.S. (1940). *Conceptions of Modern Psychiatry.* New York: W.W. Norton.

Sullivan, H.S. (1947). The study of psychiatry: Three orienting lectures. *Psychiatry*, 10: 355–371.

Sullivan, H.S. (1953). *The Interpersonal Theory of Psychiatry.* New York: Norton.

Sullivan, H.S. (1954). *The Psychiatric Interview* (eds. H.S. Perry and M.L. Gawel). New York: W.W. Norton.

Sullivan, H.S. (1956). *Clinical Studies in Psychiatry.* New York: Norton.

Sullivan, H.S. (1962). *Schizophrenia as a Human Process.* New York: W. W. Norton.

Sullivan, H.S. (1964). *The Fusion of Psychiatry and Social Science.* New York: W.W. Norton.

Sullivan, H.S. (1972). *Personal Psychopathology.* New York: Norton.

Tarnopolsky, A. (2003). The concept of dissociation in early psychoanalytic writers. *J. Trauma & Dissoc.*, 4(3): 7–25.

Thomas, W. I., and Thomas, D.S. (1928). *The Child in America: Behavior Problems and Programs.* Michigan: Johnson Reprint.

Thompson, C.M. (1949). Harry Stack Sullivan, the man. *Psychiatry*, 12, 435–437.

Thompson, C.M. (1951). *Psychoanalysis: Evolution and Development.* London: George Allen & Unwin.

Thompson, C.M. (1964). *Interpersonal Psychoanalysis: The Selected Papers of Clara M. Thompson.* M.R. Green (ed.). New York: Basic Books.

Treccani, G. (1986). *Vocabolario della lingua italiana* [Vocabulary of the Italian Language]. Milan: Arti Grafiche Ricordi.

Vargas, F. (2014). *The Ghost Riders of Ordebec: A Commissaire Adamsberg Novel.* New York: Random House. Kindle Edition.

Wilson, R.A., and Foglia, L. (2011). Embodied Cognition. In E.N. Zalta, *The Stanford Encyclopedia of Philosophy.* http://tinyurl.com/zz3nqxv.

Wolstein, B. (1954). *Transference.* New York: Grune & Stratton.

Wolstein, B. (1959). *Countertransference*. New York: Grune & Stratton.

Wolstein, B. (1997). The first direct analysis of transference and counter-transference. *Psychoanal. Inquiry*, 17, 505–521.

Yourcenar, M. (1951). *Mèmoires d'Hadrien*. Paris: Librairie Plon.

Zilboorg, G. (1933). Anxiety without affect. *Psychoanal. Quarterly*, 2, 48–67.

Zito, S. (2006). Psicoanalisi contemporanea [Contemporary psychoanalysis]. *Ricerca Psicoanalitica*, 17(3): 369–373.

Index

For Product Safety Concerns and Information please contact our EU
representative GPSR@taylorandfrancis.com
Taylor & Francis Verlag GmbH, Kaufingerstraße 24, 80331 München, Germany